Interventions
for Struggling Learners

Interventions
for Struggling Learners

PUTTING RTI INTO PRACTICE

by Gretchen Goodman

Crystal Springs
BOOKS

A division of  Staff Development for Educators

Peterborough, New Hampshire

Published by Crystal Springs Books
A division of Staff Development for Educators (SDE)
10 Sharon Road, PO Box 500
Peterborough, NH 03458
1-800-321-0401
www.crystalsprings.com
www.sde.com
© 2008 Gretchen Goodman
Illustrations © 2008 Crystal Springs Books
Published 2008
Printed in the United States of America
12 11 10 09   2 3 4 5
ISBN: 978-1-934026-18-2

Many of the strategies in this book were adapted from
I Can Learn! and *More I Can Learn!* by Gretchen Goodman.

Library of Congress Cataloging-in-Publication Data

Goodman, Gretchen.
  Interventions for struggling learners : putting RTI into practice / by
Gretchen Goodman ; illustrations by Coni Porter.
    p. cm.
  ISBN 978-1-934026-18-2
  1. Remedial teaching. 2. Individualized instruction. I. Porter,
Coni, ill. II. Title.

  LB1029.R4G65 2008
  371.39'4--dc22

  2008019380

Editor: **Elaine Ambrose**
Cover and Interior Page Design: **CPorter Designs**
Production Coordinator: **Deborah Fredericks**
Illustrated by: **Coni Porter**

==

This book is dedicated to my mother,
Marian Bubb—a strong, loving woman who has always
placed the needs of others before her own. Being independent has
been her forte for 84 years. Whenever she was told she "couldn't," she
always fought hard to prove she could.

This book is also in loving memory of my father,
Calvin Bubb, who ruled with an iron fist and a
marshmallow heart. We miss you, Poppy.

==

Table of Contents

Acknowledgments

Thank you to the many creative, dedicated teachers across
the country who have shared their successful strategies and great
ideas with me and other participants in my seminars.

Many thanks to my RTI gurus, Dr. Joseph Kovaleski
and Dr. David Lillenstein. These two brilliant men understand
children, psychology, special services, and effective teaching and
collaboration better than anyone I know. Thank you both for
being my mentors and my personal "ask Jeeves." You are making a
difference for children all across the country.

A big thanks also to Elaine Ambrose, who is much more
than an editor. Elaine has never forgotten her roots as an
educator or her desire to help all children succeed.

Introduction

Response to Intervention, or RTI, is about helping every child succeed and improving the quality of education for all children. It involves screening and preassessment, responsive and diagnostic teaching, and progress monitoring, with an emphasis on early intervention. The classroom teacher is, as always, at the heart of learning, but RTI demands as well the involvement of all staff members in a school—everyone is a stakeholder in each child's success. Since the passage of the Individuals with Disabilities Education Act (IDEA) in 2004, RTI has become a model for collaboration among general education teachers, special education staff, literacy and reading coaches, psychologists, guidance counselors, principals, and other specialists.

The status quo, wait-to-fail model has run its course. No Child Left Behind charges schools with the responsibility to make sure each child makes measurable yearly progress, and Response to Intervention is a growing movement to meet that charge. RTI is also about qualifying the right students for special education services.

RTI is not waiting for the school psychologist to test an at-risk student or waiting for the student to fail. Teachers don't have to wait for a discrepancy between IQ (ability) and performance (achievement) to surface or wait until third grade to see if a student "grows out of it." With its emphasis on grades K

WHAT THE RESEARCH SAYS

The research assures us that almost every student can learn if

- instructional strategies are differentiated to meet students' needs

- lessons align with the student's preferred learning style

- teachers are well trained

- a high-quality, research-based core curriculum is in place and is taught with fidelity by all teachers in a school district

Core RTI Principles

- **All students can learn.**

- **Early intervention is best.**

- **Instruction and intervention are multi-tiered.**

- **Problem-solving models are used.**

- **Instruction and assessment are scientifically validated.**

- **Universal screening and progress monitoring inform instruction.**

- **Decision-making is data-based.**

- **Assessment drives instruction.**

through 4 reading, writing, math, and behavior, RTI is a multi-tiered model to develop and implement coordinated, early intervening strategies for at-risk learners who have not been identified as needing special education or related services. These "gray-area" students are the ones who often fall between the cracks without additional support.

Using RTI, teachers provide instruction and intervention that is matched to a student's specific, identified needs. Teachers who use differentiated instructional strategies are already facilitating learning by providing responsive, student-centered teaching. The next step is to adopt systematic ways to assess and monitor each child's progress, and then to respond appropriately when progress is not made. Child-response data is used to make changes in instruction for students who haven't reached benchmarks or proficiency standards.

In early fall, comprehensive, universal screenings are used to identify at-risk learners who need additional support. Results drive instruction for these learners who have different needs and readiness levels. Additional screenings in winter and spring track student progress and identify any other students who aren't making the expected gains. At-risk students need even more frequent monitoring to determine which interventions are effective. Your school may use DIBELS, 4Sight, STAR, or another tool for benchmark and progress monitoring. These and other assessments used by classroom teachers—the first line of intervention—should identify precisely where an at-risk student's confusions and weaknesses lie. Teachers then use research-based instruction aligned with the student's learning style to target her weaknesses. Every child's progress is monitored, but those students who are at risk for failure come under the closest scrutiny. All students will benefit from high-quality instruction that includes scientific, research-based reading and math programs and timely interventions when needed. RTI is a powerful model for delivering interventions that can prevent failure.

RTI brings together general, remedial, and special education teachers to document and provide effective education. Early intervening services dovetail with differentiated instructional techniques. Multi-tiered models of intervention with scientifically validated instruction and assessment increase success for struggling learners. Together, assessment screening, diagnostic testing, and progress monitoring all inform and drive instruction. For RTI to be successful, a school must have in place the following:

- universal screening
- progress monitoring
- careful data management
- collaboration and teaming
- time built into the schedule to discuss children
- administrative support
- differentiated instructional strategies
- on-going staff development

A Three-Tiered Model

> ## FIRST AND FOREMOST . . .
>
> The school district must provide health screenings to rule out hearing, vision, and other health problems that could hinder a child's ability to learn. Other issues that may pose barriers to learning include difficult home situations such as separation, divorce, an incarcerated parent or sibling, and health issues of other family members, as well as homelessness. It's also important to know if English is the primary language spoken at home. If possible, have the school social worker, psychologist, or guidance counselor meet with the student or family to rule out stressors at home that might impact school success. Ideally, the occupational therapist, physical therapist, and physical education teacher would also assess the child's motor skills and suggest interventions if needed.

Tier 1

Tier I is general education instruction, using research-based, scientifically validated curricula, with regular progress monitoring of students. In Tier 1, teachers and support staff collaborate to gather data on student performance, analyze it to identify which students have gaps in skills, set measurable goals for closing the gaps, and choose or create instructional strategies. Approximately 80 to 85 percent of students experience success within Tier 1 when their teachers supplement comprehensive reading programs and math instruction with differentiated instructional strategies. The general education classroom is the first line of intervention. All students in the general education classroom are exposed to the core curriculum that has been mandated by a school district in Tier 1, as well as in Tiers 2 and 3, and some students will need to be taught the curriculum more than once.

Tier 2

Tier 2 involves more intensive and specific instruction directed at students who have not met benchmarks, according to the results of universal screening. Tier 2 instruction is delivered in addition to strong Tier 1 teaching, not in place of it. A student's diagnosed weakness is targeted in Tier 2. Usually, a small group of students (no more than four) with similar deficits in skills receives direct, inten-

Most States Are Using a Three-Tiered Model

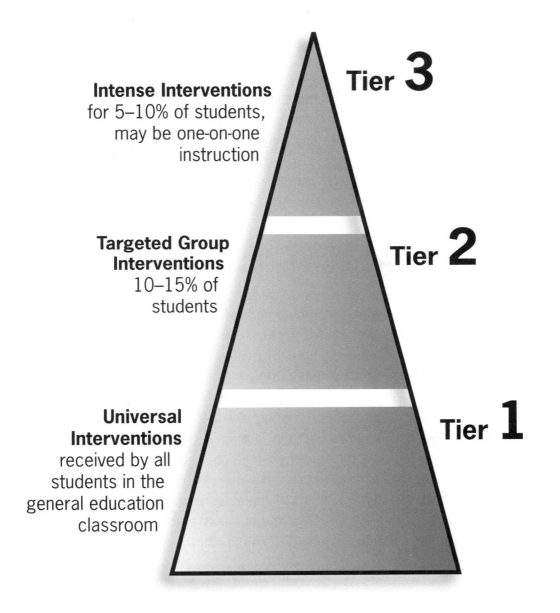

Intense Interventions for 5–10% of students, may be one-on-one instruction

Tier **3**

Targeted Group Interventions 10–15% of students

Tier **2**

Universal Interventions received by all students in the general education classroom

Tier **1**

All students receive instruction based on the school district's mandated core programs in reading and mathematics, which are research-based and scientifically validated.

sive instruction for 20 to 30 minutes a day, 3 to 5 days a week, for at least 10 to 12 weeks. This small group instruction must include

- reteaching to mastery
- immediate, corrective feedback
- more time on difficult tasks
- strategies tailored to the at-risk learners

Progress of Tier 2 students is monitored *at least* twice a month using quick assessment tools to measure improvement. When improvement is not noted, instruction needs to change. Tier 2 groups should be needs-based, flexible, and fluid, and students should receive differentiated instruction that scaffolds learning. Teachers and interventionists must keep careful records and must note the results of the interventions they use with individual students, along with the progress monitoring data.

When improvement is not noted, instruction needs to change.

Even with targeted intervention, some students still lose ground. That's when classroom teachers share the results of their interventions with colleagues, and additional instructional options are investigated. A student-intervention team generally consists of the principal, nurse, school psychologist, guidance counselor, reading specialist, and other learning specialists. As a result of the team's collaboration, students may receive supplemental instruction from Title I, the reading specialist, a teacher of English for Speakers of Other Languages (ESOL), special education staff, interventionist, coaches, and others. This generally smaller percentage of students receives instruction that aligns with the teacher's classroom instruction for 20 to 30 minutes, several days a week, if not every day. Again, careful records of interventions used and student results are kept, both to guide instruction and to determine whether more intensive instruction is needed.

Tier 3

Tier 3 intervention is directed at the smaller percentage of students, generally 5 to 10 percent, who fail to respond to Tier 2 instructional interventions, based on frequent progress monitoring assessment. Instruction is delivered to individual students in Tier 3 either in the general education classroom or in another location. Student progress is assessed more frequently. Tier 3 interventions should be carefully monitored by a team, and a special education evaluation or referral may be made while the student is receiving this instruction. A student who still doesn't make academic gains after a reasonable period of time receives more intensive individual support, again with accurate record-keeping and formal progress monitoring assessments to determine outcomes and next steps. When a student does not progress at an adequate rate with this intense level of intervention, he might be referred for special education services.

How to Use This Book

Learning to read is the most critical aspect of education at the early primary level. More young students fall between the cracks because of problems learning to read than any other academic issue. Therefore, the sections on reading in this book are the most heavily represented. Many of these strategies can be adapted for use in writing and math, too, and where that's the case, this has been noted.

The strategies and activities in this book represent best practices. They have been classroom-tested and they are student-approved. However, they are intended to be used to support the scientifically validated, research-based reading and math core programs that your school district has mandated. Organized by skill area, these strategies are designed to help you differentiate your instruction to meet the various learning styles of the students in your classes.

More young students fall between the cracks because of problems learning to read than any other academic issue.

Although behavioral issues that interfere with academic success are not addressed in this book, many teachers find that when the right match between a student and a method of instruction is made, and the child begins to enjoy academic success, some behavioral problems do, in fact, decrease. (One note of caution—some of the strategies and activities presented here include the use of food as a manipulative or learning aid. Always be aware of possible food sensitivities or allergies among your students and have non-food substitutes available to use instead.)

A Note About Learning Styles

Most children have a preferred learning style that reflects the way or ways in which they process information most efficiently. Some people even use different learning styles in different situations, and most of us have different degrees of preference when it comes to how we like to learn. Presenting new information to a child in her preferred learning style helps her to process it and reduces frustration. Learning styles grow, evolve, and change just like children do, so it's wise to re-evaluate students every few years. Once you know what a child's preferred learning style is, it's important to provide activities that target her learning style, but it's also wise to offer plenty of different activities to develop other learning styles as well. The strategies presented in this book make it easy to do just that.

Learning styles are generally classified as auditory, visual, and tactile-kinesthetic. Most people, if asked to think about a cat, for example, either see the animal's image in their minds, hear a purr or a meow, or think about soft fur under their hands. Simply put, those who call up a mental image of the animal are more likely to be visual learners, those who hear the sounds a cat might make may have a preference for auditory learning, and people who imagine the feel of the cat's fur under their hands may have a preference for tactile-kinesthetic learning.

You can often determine a child's preferred learning style just by doing some good old-fashioned kid-watching and talking to parents about their children.

Generally speaking, auditory learners tend to

- chat or hum to themselves when they are trying to learn something new
- like discussions and having directions explained to them orally
- enjoy listening to stories and songs on tape
- learn better when they can read the material to themselves

Children who are primarily visual learners

- want to see what it is they have to learn
- can recall the details in a picture or diagram
- can usually follow written directions well
- often have good eye-hand coordination

Tactile-kinesthetic learners are your movers and shakers, literally. These are the children (and the adults!) who

- jiggle their feet and tap their pencils to help them learn
- have to handle things and try them out to process new information
- may "talk" with their hands
- might need frequent breaks

The learning styles assessment reproducible that is included on page 166 is informal and can be administered to a student by an aide or other support staff. Most children enjoy being asked the questions and may gain insight into themselves as learners.

In *Interventions for Struggling Learners*, you'll notice that many of the strategies have a symbol of an ear, an eye, a shoe, or a combination of these symbols. These indicate that a strategy is particularly well suited for students whose primary learning style is auditory, visual, or tactile-kinesthetic.

 = auditory

= visual

 = tactile-kinesthetic

In addition, many of the strategies in this book are also effective as anchor activities that students can work on if they are not meeting with you and their assigned work has been completed. A vital component of a successful RTI program is small group and individual intensive reteaching. Therefore, carefully considered and planned anchor activities are an important part of RTI. The anchor activities should be engaging and interesting, and they should offer students opportunities to reinforce and extend their understanding of concepts that have been taught. Ideally, anchor activities should give students choices that address their individual learning styles. Effective anchor activities also have a self-assessment or self-correction component so that students do not have to interrupt a teacher who is delivering an intervention strategy to a small group or individual. Strategies and activities throughout this book that can also be used as anchor activities are designated with the illustration of an anchor.

⚓ = anchor activity

RTI Documentation Folders

Each of the strategies and activities in this book is marked with a code that you can use if you are completing an intervention documentation folder on a student's academic needs. These number and letter codes are simply for your convenience. You can write the name of an intervention strategy you have tried with a student if you prefer. The codes consist of the first two letters of the section in which the strategy is located (or in some cases, the initial letters of the section title, such as SP for Sentences and Paragraphs) and the number of the strategy. For example, PH–12 refers to the twelfth strategy in the phonics section. In the table of contents, you'll find the letter code for each section in parentheses after the section title. Using the codes, it's easy to note which DI (Differentiated Instruction) strategies you have already tried with a student.

If you don't have these folders from Crystal Springs Books, you can use the reproducible on page 168 to track intervention strategies you have used with an at-risk learner and monitor the student's progress.

BENEFITS OF RTI

- RTI addresses the academic weaknesses of at-risk learners before they fail.

- It ensures that poor academic performance is not a result of poor instruction.

- The regular ed classroom is the first line of intervention.

- RTI merges regular, remedial, and special ed for student success.

- Assessments and interventions are closely linked.

- Child-response data drives instruction.

- Differentiated intervention strategies and attention to learning styles improve academic outcomes for all students.

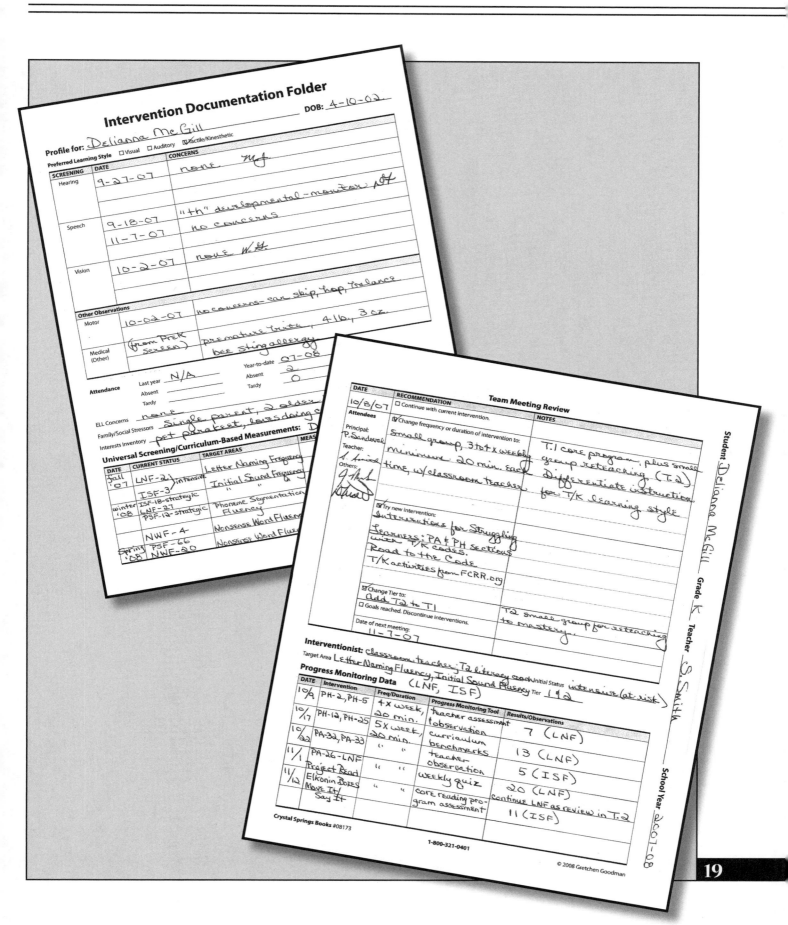

Intervention Documentation Folder   DOB: 4-10-02

Profile for: Delianna McGill

Preferred Learning Style: ☐ Visual ☐ Auditory ☑ Tactile/Kinesthetic

SCREENING	DATE	CONCERNS
Hearing	9-27-07	none MJ
Speech	9-18-07	"th" developmental—monitor NY
	11-7-07	no concerns
Vision	10-2-07	none W.H.

Other Observations

Motor	10-02-07	no concerns—can skip, hop, balance
Medical (Other)	(from PreK screen)	premature birth, 4 lb, 3 oz. bee sting allergy

Attendance
Last year: N/A   Year-to-date 07-08
Absent: ___   Absent: 2
Tardy: ___   Tardy: 0

ELL Concerns: none
Family/Social Stressors: Single parent, 2 older...
Interests Inventory: pet parakeet, loves doing...

Universal Screening/Curriculum-Based Measurements:

DATE	CURRENT STATUS	TARGET AREAS	MEAS...
fall 07	LNF-2, intensive	Letter Naming Frequency	
	ISF-3-strategic	Initial Sound Frequency	
winter 08	ISF-18-strategic	Phoneme Segmentation Fluency	
	LNF-27 PSF-12-strategic		
	NWF-4	Nonsense Word Fluency	
Spring '08	PSF-66 NWF-20	Nonsense Word Fluency	

Team Meeting Review

Student: Delianna McGill   Grade: K   Teacher: S. Smith   School Year: 2007-08

DATE	RECOMMENDATION	NOTES
10/8/07	☐ Continue with current intervention.	
Attendees	☑ Change frequency or duration of intervention to:	
Principal: P. Sandoval	small group, 3 to 4x weekly	T-1 core program, plus small group reteaching (T.2)
Teacher: S. Smith	minimum 20 min. each time, w/classroom teacher	Differentiate instruction for T/K learning style
Others: J.A...		
	☑ Try new intervention: Interventions for Struggling Learners: PA & PH sections with T/K codes. Road to the Code T/K activities from FCRR.org	
	☑ Change Tier to: add T2 to T1	T2 small group for reteaching to mastery.
	☐ Goals reached. Discontinue interventions.	
Date of next meeting: 11-7-07		

Interventionist: classroom teacher; T2 literacy coach
Target Area: Letter Naming Fluency, Initial Sound Fluency (LNF, ISF)   Initial Status: intensive (at-risk)   Tier 1 & 2

Progress Monitoring Data

DATE	Intervention	Freq/Duration	Progress Monitoring Tool	Results/Observations
10/9	PH-2, PH-5	4x week 20 min.	teacher assessment t observation	7 (LNF)
10/17	PH-12, PH-25	5x week 20 min.	curriculum benchmarks	13 (LNF)
10/22	PA-32, PA-33	" "	teacher observation	5 (ISF)
11/1	PA-26-LNF Project Read	" "	weekly quiz	20 (LNF) continue LNF as review in T.2
11/12	Elkonin Boxes Move It! Say It	" "	core reading program assessment	11 (ISF)

Crystal Springs Books #08173

1-800-321-0401

© 2008 Gretchen Goodman

READING

Phonemic Awareness (PA)

Phonics (PH)

Fluency (FL)

Vocabulary (VO)

Comprehension (CO)

General Strategies for Reading Success

- Fill your classroom library with a wide variety of written materials. Besides storybooks, include nonfiction books, brochures for fun places to visit, children's magazines and other periodicals, posters with captions, riddle and joke books, cookbooks written for children, the kids' comics section from the Sunday newspaper, craft books, children's atlases, and even maps.

- Survey children about their reading preferences. You can do this orally with younger children. With older students, put up a piece of chart paper in your classroom and ask children to add subjects or topics that they want to read about. If a student sees a show about sharks, for example, that's a topic he may be excited about and he'll be motivated to read more about them.

- Let children read all over the room. Some will be comfortable reading at their desks, while others may need to stretch out on the rug, curl up in a beanbag chair, or rock in the classroom rocking chair as they read.

- Make good literature available on tape for auditory learners.

- Invite guests to your room to read to students so they see that their local heroes such as firefighters and rescue personnel are also book lovers. You can either offer the guest a book ahead of time that you know children will love or let them bring their own favorite.

- Have wordless books available. Encourage struggling readers to tell you the story as they turn the pages and study the pictures. You'll find lists of wonderful wordless books on the Internet.

- If you use monthly book-club catalogs in your room, turn all your points into more books. Write students' names on Popsicle sticks and put them in a jar. Every month, pull out three sticks and invite the children whose names are on them to pick a title from the catalog to add to the classroom library. Set a dollar limit and allow books only. When your order arrives, those three students get first chance to read the books they chose.

- Teach and model good prereading strategies such as looking at the cover and the illustrations, reading the "blurb" or chapter titles, and taking the time to make connections to the book.

Phonemic Awareness

Stretch It
PA–1

Use a wide piece of elastic or an exercise band for this segmentation fluency activity. (If your school has a physical therapist who comes in to work with children, she may be able to give you a few yards of the stretchy elastic that is used for P.T. exercises.) Attach a picture card or letters to the band. Have students stretch the sounds as they stretch the elastic. The word *bike* becomes /b/ ... /i/ ... /k/ and students can identify each phoneme they hear. This is fun to do with mini slinkies as well. Do the same activity with syllables to help students hear the different sound chunks in words. If you have bands or mini slinkies in a basket at your writing center, students can use them to help them spell words they are writing independently.

Buy It!
PA–2

Give your students plastic pennies or toy dollar bills. (See p. 169 for a reproducible you can use for "funny money.") They will give you a coin or a bill for each phoneme in a word. Say a word such as *time*. Have the children pay you a penny or dollar for each phoneme they hear in the word. They should give you three pennies or dollars for the three phonemes in *time*. (They could also deposit the coins in a piggy bank as they say the segments, in case they don't want to let go of their money!)

Marshmallows in a Cup
PA-3 🖎

Give students real cups of hot chocolate and mini marshmallows for this strategy or use empty mugs and cotton balls for marshmallows if food sensitivities are a concern. Say a word or nonsense word, such as *mup*, and have students repeat it and drop a marshmallow or cotton ball into their mugs for each phoneme they say.

Segment Caterpillar
PA-4 👁

Make a copy of the reproducible segmented caterpillar on page 170, cut it into three parts, and laminate each part. Have the student hand you or point to the phoneme you say. If you say the word *pit*, for example, and ask the student to give you the part of the caterpillar that says /t/, he should give you the last segment.

Who's on First?
PA-5

Place three cards with animals on them in front of the student. If you lay out cards with a goat, a pig, and a duck, you would ask your student to:

1. identify the animals
2. tell you which one begins with a certain sound (for example, which one begins with /d/?)
3. tell you which one ends with a certain sound (for example, which one ends with /g/?)

Next, point to one card, say the word, and ask, "What's the first sound you hear? What sound do you hear last?" Use a timer to improve fluency.

Bull's-eye Circles
PA-6 🔲

Place pictures or picture cards on the different rings of a bull's-eye target that you set on the floor, or purchase a Velcro set from a dollar store. Have each student in turn toss a Velcro ball or a small beanbag onto the target. The student tells you what picture or pictures are in the ring his ball landed in and then he says a rhyming word for each one. Accept nonsense words, too. If his ball lands in a ring that has a picture of a table, he might give you the nonsense word *wable*.

Elkonin Boxes
PA-7 🔲 👁

Show the student a picture, such as a picture of a key. Below the picture, draw two square boxes. Ask the student what sound goes in each box. He should tell you that /k/ goes in the box on the left and /e/ (the long sound of the letter *e*) goes in the box on the right. Later, have more boxes than there are phonemes in the word. If you show a picture of a pie and you have three boxes beneath it, can the student tell you that only the first two boxes are needed? Vary the activities by having the student color in boxes that represent certain phonemes. For example, you might show him a picture of a rug and ask him to color the /r/ green and the /g/ yellow.

Listen and Clap
PA-8 🔲

Since many students come to school without having heard or learned nursery rhymes, this strategy does double duty. Read or recite nursery rhymes aloud and have your students clap their hands when they hear a word you have asked them to listen for. If you have asked them to listen for the word *peep*, they should clap when you say that word in the nursery rhyme Little Bo Peep.

Later, read the same rhymes but have them clap when they hear a word that rhymes with a word you select. If you say, "Listen for words that rhyme with *toy*," they should clap when they hear *boy* (Little Boy Blue), for example.

Popcorn Party
PA-9 [C]

To have students practice segmenting words into phonemes, give them each three or four pieces of popcorn. Direct them to lay out their pieces of popcorn for each sound they hear in a word you will say. For example, if you say the word *time*, they should lay out three pieces, one for /t/, one for /i/, and one for /m/. Then, they take away and eat specific "segments" according to your directions. For example, if you ask students to lay out the word *speak* with their popcorn pieces, they should lay out four pieces of popcorn, one for each phoneme in the word. If you ask them to eat the /p/, they should each eat the second piece. If you say, "Eat the /k/ sound," they should eat the last piece.

Turkeys on the Trot
PA-10 [C] [S]

This strategy is fun all year, but especially in November. Put a piece of tape across the table to mark a finish line and use plastic turkeys (or other animals) that the child moves toward the finish line as you say words in segments. So if the word is *pie*, for example, the child will need two turkeys. If you say /p/, she moves the first turkey toward the finish line. When you say /i/, she moves the second turkey. Give her a new word and additional turkeys if needed, and try this again.

You can also do this with syllables in a word. If you say *November*, the child lines up three turkeys, one for each syllable. When you say /ber/, the third turkey moves toward the finish line and when you say /vem/, the second turkey moves.

Turtle Talk
PA-11 [C]

To give students practice blending sounds to form words, talk like a turtle would. Say a word slowly and drawn out, leaving about a half-second between each phoneme. Can your student blend the sounds together to tell you what word you said? If you say /p/ . . . /a/ . . . /per/, can the student give you back the word *paper*?

Segment Switch
PA-12

Work with students in groups of three to five for practice segmenting words into their individual phonemes. Give the students in the group a set of letter cards that includes vowels. Segment a word, such as *bike*, and have students line up according to the sounds they hear in the word: /b/ /i/ /k/. Make sure they are lining up in the correct direction, starting on the left with *b* and moving to the right with *i* and *k*.

Tap and Sweep
PA-13

To help students learn letter sounds and practice blending them to make words or nonsense words, try this. Write the letters on the board or use plastic letters on a table. Tap each one and have the student make the sound of each. So if your word is *pat*, you'll have *p*, *a*, and *t* written on the board or placed on the table, and as you tap the *p*, your student makes the sound of that letter, then you tap the *a*, and he makes the sound of the letter, and finally you tap the *t* and the student responds with /t/. Then move your finger back to the first letter, in this case *p*, and sweep it beneath all three letters while the student blends the sounds to form the word *pat*.

PHONEMIC AWARENESS

Phonemic awareness is the ability to hear and manipulate sounds in words. Before they can read, children must be aware of how sounds work in words. Children who have developed phonemic awareness recognize beginning sounds. They can tell you the first or last sound they hear in a word and are able to blend separate sounds together to say a real word or a nonsense word. They can also chunk or segment words into their separate phonemes. They can tell you when words rhyme and when they don't. Help children develop these skills with activities that have them manipulate sounds by taking away or adding phonemes to create words, blending sounds to make real words as well as nonsense words, and listening for and creating rhymes, and segmenting phonemes. Make the activities fun. Young children need frequent opportunities to play with the language in order to develop phonemic awareness skills.

Auto Races
PA-14

Draw four race cars on big sheets of oak tag and number them 1, 2, 3, and 4. Say a word and direct the student to run and stand on the race car with the number that's the same as the number of phonemes in the word. So if you say *camp*, he runs to the number 4 car. Make a checkered flag out of black and white construction paper. The student thinks about the real or nonsense word you said while he waits for the signal to go.

Use this strategy with syllables, too. Can your student discern the number of syllables he hears in the word *elephant* and run to the number 3 car?

Roll and Say
PA-15

Use a small, soft ball for this exercise. Have students sit in a circle on the floor or at a table with their chairs pushed in to keep the ball from rolling onto the floor. Say a word such as *lake* and roll the ball to any student, who must say the first sound, /l/. She rolls it to another student, who gives the second sound, /a/. This student rolls the ball to a third student, who adds the /k/ sound heard at the end of the word. Have pictures that match the words handy for students who forget what they are trying to segment or need a visual representation of the word.

Point to Show First or Last
PA-16

Students practice distinguishing between initial and final consonants with this strategy. Give the student a picture card, such as one with a picture of a pig. Also give him two blocks plus an arrow cut from oak tag. Ask him to use the arrow to point to the block that represents the /p/ sound and then point to the block that stands for the /g/ sound.

Cube Moves
PA–17 🔥

To help a student manipulate the phonemes she hears in a word, give her a Unifix cube or other cube to represent each phoneme. For example, for the word *dog,* you would give her three cubes. After she has touched each cube while saying the phonemes in the word dog, /d/ /o/ /g/, ask her which cube she would need to replace to turn the word *dog* into *fog.* Which cube would need to be replaced to turn *fog* into *fig*? Then ask her which one she would need to replace if she wanted to turn *fig* into *fit*, and so on.

Sliding Sounds
PA–18 🔊 👁 🔥

Use magnetic letters and a cookie sheet for this activity. Have the letters that represent the sounds your student is working on at the top of the cookie sheet. As you say a phoneme, he slides the letter down. For example, if you have the letters *p, h, a, o, s, t,* and *m* on the cookie sheet and you slowly say or segment the word *past*, he will first slide down the *p*, then the *a*, then the *s*, and finally the *t*. Review the word by tapping each letter as he says each sound and sweeping your finger underneath all four letters for your student to say the word *past* fluently. Caution: At the bottom of the sheet, have a green sticker dot to indicate where the student is to place the first letter or sound. This keeps him from laying words down backwards and reinforces the concept of print being read from left to right.

Duck, Duck, Rhyme
PA–19 🔊 🔥

Give the student who is "it" a card with a picture on it, such as a ball. He walks around tapping the others who must repeat his word, *ball*. When he taps a student and says, "Rhyme it!" that student must quickly say a word that rhymes with *ball* and chase the tapper. If she tags him, he sits and she becomes "it." Accept rhyming nonsense words as well as real words.

Puppy Chow
PA-20 [C] [S]

Use a little plastic doggy dish and small dog biscuits for this activity. Line up the treats to represent the segments of the word you are going to say. For example, if you said *rat*, you would line up three treats. Then ask the student to put the /t/ in the dog dish. Ask him to tell you what is left. Ask him to put /r/ in the dish and tell you what is left.

For compound words, say a word such as *snowman* and have the student place a biscuit for each syllable in front of the dog dish. Ask your student to put *snow* in the dog dish and tell you what is left. Use the same strategy for syllables in a word, too. If you say *umbrella*, can your student place three treats in front of the dog dish for the three syllables in the word? If you ask him to put *um* in the dish, can he tell you what is left?

Rhyming Word Chairs
PA-21 [C] [S]

Have students arrange their chairs in a circle, then remove one chair. Have them walk around in a circle outside the chairs as you say a series of words that rhyme. Tell them that when you say a word that doesn't rhyme with the others, they should sit in a chair as quickly as they can. Rather than calling a child out and removing a chair, keep playing for lots of fun and practice. Include nonsense words, too.

Beat the Drum
PA-22 [C] [S]

Give one student a small drum. (You might be able to borrow one from the music teacher in your school.) Have her call on a friend to say the name of a brother or sister. The drummer girl beats out the syllables in the name. If the name given is *Jonathan*, she taps three beats on the drum. Have her also say each syllable as she taps the drum.

Ditch It
PA-23 👁 ✏ 👂

Place three objects, such a hat, a picture of a horse, and a plastic pig in front of the student. His job is to pick out the one that doesn't have the same beginning sound as the others. Vary the activity by asking about ending sounds, initial blends, consonant digraphs, and more, according to what the individual student needs to work on. If you have a whole box of plastic farm or zoo animals, this is more fun for students and easier for you since you don't need to gather a collection of items.

Cut It Out!
PA-24 👁 ✏

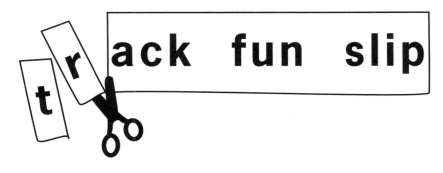

Give students sentence strips with real or nonsense words written on them and a pair of scissors each. If the first word is *track*, ask them to cut off the /t/ and tell you what's left. Then ask them to cut off /r/ and have them say the nonsense word *ack*. You might ask them to put back the /t/ sound and tell you what word they have (*tack*) before going to the second word on the strip and doing the same kinds of exercises.

Say It
PA-25 👂

Can your student hear and manipulate phonemes to create new words or nonsense words? Ask the student to say a word such as *break*. Then ask him to say it without the /b/. He should say *rake*. Say *crash*; can he say it without the /cr/? He should say *ash*. Then go the other way, having your student add a phoneme to create a new word. Ask him to say *all*; then ask him to say it with /b/ at the beginning. He should say *ball*.

What Did I Write?
PA-26 ⬚

Write a letter on your student's back slowly with your finger and ask her to tell you the sound of the letter you wrote. Ask her to tell you the letter. Write three letters for a CVC word and see if she can blend them to tell you the word. This can also be done with partners writing on each other's backs for a group or whole-class activity.

First and second graders will also enjoy this activity. Student one gets a set of cards containing letters, numerals, sight words, or spelling words. He slowly traces the number, word, or letter on his partner's back. The partner must identify what was traced. Partners then switch roles. Another way to do this is to have students use small, dry watercolor paintbrushes to "paint" the letter or number on their partner's hand or arm.

Listen and Flash
PA-27 ⬚

Give each student three cards on which you've written the numbers 1, 2, and 3 in black marker. Say a word and have students hold up the card with the number that represents the number of phonemes or syllables they heard in your word, depending on the skill you are targeting. This is also a quick way to assess students and find out who needs additional practice.

Popcorn Readers
PA-28 ⬚

Cut large popcorn shapes out of oak tag and on each one write a different letter or sound your students are working on, one phoneme or letter to each piece of "popcorn." Distribute them. Line three students up and have them pop up to read their sounds. If you line up the students with the popcorn shapes marked with *l, i,* and *p,* they should pop up in sequence to say /l/, then /i/, then /p/, and finally they all pop up together once more to say the word *lip.* Remind them to go from left to right, the way we read words in print.

Egg Scramble
PA–29

Have students drop jelly beans into egg-carton cups for each segment or sound in a word or nonsense word. If you say the nonsense word *slike*, for example, they would drop four beans into four egg-carton cups as they segment the nonsense word into /s/, /l/, /i/, and /k/. This is fun to do around Easter time, although students will enjoy it any time, especially if they can eat some of the "sounds" when they have finished the lesson. Later, use the same strategy for teaching students to chunk words into syllables.

Phoneme Toss
PA–30

For groups working on phonemes, try this strategy. Use a white foam cube or make your own. (See the cube pattern reproducible on p. 171.) Write a number on each side of the cube from 1 to 4. You'll repeat two numbers in order to cover all six sides of the cube. Students toss the cube and think of a word that has the same number of sounds as the number that's on top. So if the cube lands with 3 on top, a student may say the word *cup* with three phonemes. Make this more challenging by asking students to create only nonsense words.

Use the same strategy for syllables in words. If a student tosses the cube and it lands with a 4 on top, he has to try to think of a word with four sylla-bles, such as *unusual*. If he can't come up with a word, he should ask other students for help.

Guess My Word
PA–31

When a student needs practice blending syllables to say a word, try this strategy. Say a word with more than one syllable, but say each syllable separately and pause for a half-second between each one. For example, for *Spiderman*, say /Spi/ . . . /der/ . . . /man/ and see if she can blend the syllables together to give you the word.

Mother, May I?
PA–32 🕮 🖎

Say a word and ask your student to identify the beginning sound or end sound. If she is correct, she asks, "Mother, may I?" and takes two steps. Older students can define or spell words, then take two steps after saying, "Mother, may I?"

Fill My Footprints
PA–33 🕮 🖎

Cut large footprints from chart paper or oak tag and place them on the floor, one in front of the other. Say a word and have the student jump from one footprint to the next as you say the phonemes in a word or nonsense word. You might say the nonsense word *blat*, and she would jump onto the first footprint to say /b/, then jump to the second one and say /l/, then to the third for /a/, and to the last footprint for /t/. Ask her to jump to the /a/ then to the /t/. Then ask her to jump to /b/ and so on. If you direct her to jump from /b/ to /a/ to /t/, can she blend these sounds together to tell you the word *bat*?

Use this strategy for words in a sentence to practice sequencing and fluency as well as for hearing syllables in words.

Phonics

Handy Decoding
PH–1 👁

Teach students this five-finger strategy for attacking unknown words. Draw a large outline of a hand on poster board. On each finger, write a different cue for word attack. Teach the steps in a little jingle for easier recall; the B-I-N-G-O tune works well. Display this reference chart where students can see it when they are reading and be sure to model it with students in groups and individually and have students practice it with your assistance. You can also create a bookmark with the cues for students to have when they are reading independently.

- Pinkie = Bleep. Look at the rest of the sentence for context clues while you say bleep inside your head for the mystery word.

- Ring finger = Frame. Using two fingers, make a frame around the word and study it to see if you can tell what it is.

- Middle finger = Pull Apart. Look at the word's structure. Can you see a root word, a prefix, or a suffix? Can you chunk the mystery word into syllables?

- Index finger = Sound Out. Try to pronounce the letter sounds in the word.

- Thumb = Help! Ask a buddy, your teacher, or look in a dictionary.

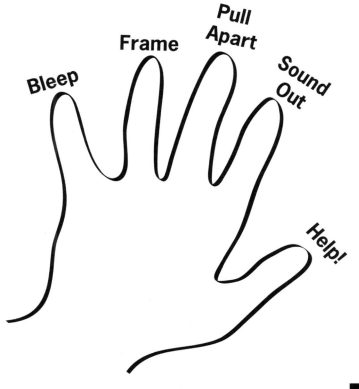

Keyboard It
PH-2 🔲 👁

For students who need to work on letter naming fluency, try this appealing strategy. Collect used keyboards from your school's technology department when computers are updated. Have students tap the letters you call out. Vary this by calling out the letters for nonsense CVC words or real words. After they have located and tapped the letters, can they tell you the word?

If you can't get keyboards, use a picture of a keyboard. (See p. 177 for a reproducible.) One advantage to this method is that children can color letters in as you say them and then see the letters you called and give you the word. You'll need to switch colors for each new word.

Fishing for Words
PH-3 🔲

Make a fishing pole out of a dowel, a piece of string, and a small magnet. Cut out a variety of oak-tag fish (or use the reproducible on p. 172) and laminate them. Attach a small, metal paper clip to each fish, along with a picture representing each new word or the word written on the fish. When a student catches a fish, she must say the word, define it, rhyme it, or spell the word that matches the picture on the fish.

Use this popular old favorite with math facts, comprehension questions, and more.

PHONICS

Phonics is about the relationships between the letters of the alphabet and the individual sounds in language. Understanding these relationships between graphemes and phonemes enables children to read and write words. The alphabetic principle gives them a system for how to encode and decode words. An understanding of phonics improves children's word recognition and reading comprehension. Children need many opportunities to practice what they are learning about letters and sounds and to apply this knowledge to words, sentences, and stories.

Vowel Power
PH-4 👁 ✍

Using letter cards or plastic letters, give a student several consonants and a vowel (for example, *o*). Ask her to build the word *mom*, then ask her to build *mop*, *now*, and *Tom*. Change the *o* to *a* and have her continue making letter substitutions and building words.

Hidden Treasure
PH-5 ✍

Hide foam or plastic alphabet letters in a small sand pail or dishpan filled with rice, dried beans, or birdseed. Ask your student to find a letter and identify it by feeling its shape. When he has found all the letters you have hidden, ask him to arrange them in the correct alphabetical order.

Run and Write
PH-6 ✍

Write a word family such as *ake* on a magnetic white board twice and have a variety of magnetic letters at the bottom of the board for children to use. Divide students into two teams. Call out a word, for example, *cake*. The two students who are first in line race to the board and add a magnetic *c* to *ake*. They then go to the end of their lines. If you don't have a magnetic white board, just have them write the onset letter or letters on the marker board or chalkboard. Award a point to the winning team for each round if you wish.

Birthday Candles
PH-7 👁 ✍

When a student has trouble sounding out phonetic words fluently, write them on a cutout of a birthday cake with candles on top. Show her how to sound out the words by blowing out the candles. She looks at a word and blows out the letter sounds in one breath to read the word with fluency.

Face Wash
PH-8 🎧 🖐 👁

Draw a picture of a child's happy face or use the reproducible on page 173. Make copies and laminate them. Give each student a copy and a wipe-off crayon or vis-à-vis marker. On the laminated faces, students write the letter that matches the sound you say. If you say /b/, they write *b* on the face. After you check their work, they wash the face with a damp paper towel or baby wipe.

If your students are working on phonemic awareness, try this strategy and let your students give the face measles or chicken pox. Tell the students you will say a word—*boat*, for example. They should give the face three chicken pox because there are three phonemes in *boat*: /b/ /oa/ /t/. Continue practicing and when you are done, the faces will be covered with dots. Students wash the faces with baby wipes at the end of the lesson.

⚓ In the Doghouse
PH-9 🎧 🖐

Use this activity to have students review long and short vowel sounds in words. Decorate two empty tissue boxes to look like doghouses. Label one house *Fido* for long vowels and the other one *Ruff* for short vowels. Leave the slit for tissues at the top open. Cut out a variety of dog shapes (or use the reproducible on p. 174), laminate them, and write a word on each dog with erasable crayon or a vis-à-vis marker. The child must put each dog in the correct doghouse according to the vowel sound she hears in the word written on it. Write the answers on the backs of the dogs to make this a self-checking activity for children.

⚓ Dot-to-Dot Newspapers for ABC Order
PH-10 👁

To reinforce the sequence of letters in the alphabet and practice letter recognition in authentic text, give students a section of a newspaper. (Many Sunday supplements include a section just for children and these work especially well.) Ask them to find the first uppercase *A* they see, and from this point, draw a line to a *B*, then to a *C*, and so on. Ask them to imagine or predict what their dot-to-dot pictures will resemble when they are completed. Let them use colorful fine-point markers for this activity so the letters and lines stand out. The next time you do it, have students look for lowercase letters.

Masking Tape Letters
PH-11 👁 ✎

Create large alphabet letters on the floor with colored tape or blue paint-masking tape that will stand out. As you hold up a picture, the student walks to the letter that has the same beginning sound or end sound, depending on your focus. To make letters last longer, ask students to do this in their stocking feet.

⚓ Sewing Letters and Words
PH-12 ✎

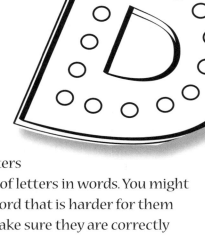

Cut a 12 x 18-inch piece of poster board into the shape of the letter or sight word a student needs to review or learn. Punch holes in the center or along the edge and have him sew the letter or word shape with yarn threaded onto a large, plastic needle (available at craft stores).

⚓ Use Your Noodle
PH-13 ✎

Ask volunteers or upper-grade students to write alphabet letters on pieces of uncooked riga-toni or macaroni. Have the students "use their noodles" and practice stringing sight words or spelling words. In addition to recognizing the letters and words, they are also practicing the sequence of letters in words. You might also have them make a noodle bracelet for one word that is harder for them to remember than others. Check their work to make sure they are correctly sequencing letters from left to right.

Touchy Letters
PH-14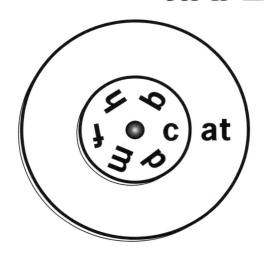

Ask students to close their eyes, and then give them a specific cardboard, wooden, foam, or plastic letter shape. Have them identify the letter by feeling its shape. You can also have them put their hands behind their backs to identify letters.

Word Family Wheels
PH-15

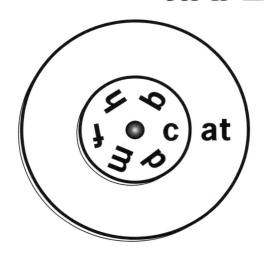

Word families can be taught in many different ways. Often children who have trouble reading and decoding respond best to the word family method. This strategy works well for sound blending. Make word wheels so only the initial consonants change. Use two circles made of oak tag, one smaller than the other. As the child rotates the top circle, he forms different words. Make sure he says each new word aloud, either to a teacher or another adult, or to a buddy who is a stronger reader. Be sure to reinforce the correct pronunciation of each word the student forms.

⚓ Alphabet Cereal
PH-16

When students need extra practice with letter recognition, give them a small bowl of alphabet cereal and ask them to match letters that are the same. Then have them find someone else in the room with those letters. Children can place their letters on a paper plate and see if they are able to match a word in their word bank or one from the word wall. Have them work with a partner to see which words they can make together. Let them eat their work at the end of the lesson. You can use alphabet pasta if you are concerned about sugar or calories. Later, have students create a silly phrase or sentence with a partner or a small group.

Configuration Spelling
PH-17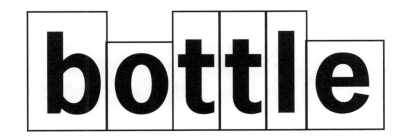

Trace the outline of sight words, spelling words, or vocabulary words on the student's paper. She fills in the correct letters by matching the configuration or shape of the word.

Cookie Spelling
PH-18

Gather small cookie sheets or metal cookie-can lids. Give the student magnetic letters that form a word family for spelling. Let him add or change only the necessary beginning letters on the tin. Check his words as you circulate or have a peer do it. Use the sheets and magnetic letters for letting students practice writing their vocabulary words, too.

Pull-Tab Words
PH-19

Here's a fun way for children to review sight words, letter blends, or rhyming words. Create posters with pull tabs in various shapes. If the students are reviewing words beginning with the letter blend *st*, create a stop sign with the letters *st* written on it, and next to the *st* a pull tab with word endings on it, such as *-op*, *-ick*, *-ep*, etc. For rhyming words, the rime stays the same and the onset, or beginning letter or letters, will be on the pull tab. So if the rime is *ame*, children will pull the tab before the rime to create words such as *tame*, *fame*, *came*, and *same*.

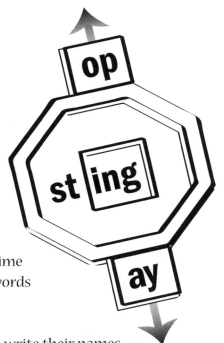

If you are using this as an anchor activity, have the children write their names on a piece of paper and record each word they create to show you later.

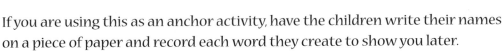

⚓ Paint Bags
PH-20 👁 🖐

This activity gives children tactile and visual reinforcement for identifying and writing letters, words, numerals, and math facts. Use a large, resealable plastic bag. Place two tablespoons of bright finger paint or hair gel inside, close the bag, and reinforce the outside edges with heavy-duty masking or duct tape to ensure that no paint leaks out. Children use the bags like magic slates. They practice writing, reading, and erasing letters, words, numbers, or math facts using soft finger pressure. They can also use a cotton swab for writing. This works better for students who use too much pressure with their fingers because the swab may bend or break if they press down too hard.

Stress to students that they must take care of their own paint bag to make it last. Write their names on the bags in permanent marker, but have them keep the bags in a central location when not in use rather than in their desks to prevent accidents.

⚓ Mix-Ups
PH-21 👂 👁 🖐

Use two shoe boxes for this activity. On index cards that you've cut in half, write all the consonants of the alphabet, as well as a variety of consonant blends, and put them in the first box. In the second box, place word families, such as *it, at, en, op, im,* and *us* that you've also written on cards. The students randomly pick a beginning letter or blend out of the first box, choose a word family card from the second box, blend the sounds, and decide if the result is a real word or a nonsense word.

If you are having children work on this independently or with a buddy, you may want to have them record all the words they form on a sheet of paper and then highlight or circle the real ones. This way you can assess their understanding later.

Before and After Bingo
PH–22

Pass out blank bingo grids and have your students write a different letter of the alphabet in each box. Then instruct them to pass their completed bingo grids two people to the right. Appoint one child to be the caller. His job is to hold up a letter card, *B* for example, for the rest to see. He then asks the students to cover a square that contains the letter *before B* in the alphabet. When one child's entire grid is covered, that student becomes the caller. The next time you play, have the caller ask students to cover a square that comes after the letter he holds up. Be sure to have alphabet desk tapes in place for students who are struggling with letter sequence.

ABC Light-Ups
PH–23 👁

Punch the shape of a letter of the alphabet into a 5 x 8-inch index card using a one-hole punch. Place the punched-out card on the overhead projector. As its holey outline is flashed onto the screen, children identify the letter or name something that begins with the letter. This is a good activity for children who need to practice letter recognition for automaticity.

⚓ Hanging around the Alphabet
PH–24 🗲 👁

String a clothesline that children can reach across the back of the room. Hang cards with the letters of the alphabet written on them on the line with pinch clothespins and have a basket with more clothespins handy for children to use. Each child searches through catalogs, magazines, or clip art, or draws a favorite picture, then hangs her picture on the line next to the letter that her picture begins with; if she clips a giraffe from a magazine, she'll hang it to the right of the letter *G*.

Letter Scavenger Hunt
PH–25

Pair students and give each team a brown paper bag with a letter written on it in marker. Let them hunt around the room to find as many objects as they can that begin with their letter and place them in the bag. The next day, repeat the activity using ending sounds. Set a timer so students remain focused on time limits for this activity. Be sure to leave time for each pair of students to show the class what they have collected and tell the others what letter each object begins with. When everyone has shared, have students put the contents of their bags back where they found them.

Jump-start the Day with Easel Letters
PH–26 👁

Paint or draw with a wide-tip marker a large outline of the letter of the day on chart paper and set it on an easel. As children arrive at school in the morning, they cut a picture out of a magazine that begins with that letter and then glue it onto the outline of the easel letter. Another way to do this is to cut a giant letter of the day out of bulletin board or butcher paper and have children decorate it. During morning meeting, you may want to review the items the children have added for accuracy. You can also have them find pictures that end with the letter of the day.

Go and Grab
PH–27

Fill two baskets with the same objects, such as crayons, markers, pencils, books, erasers, and so on, and divide the class into two teams. Have the teams form two straight lines about eight feet away from their respective baskets. Call and show a letter. The first student from each team walks quickly (or runs, if you do this outside) to her team's basket, finds the item that begins with the letter you called, and takes it back to her team. She goes to the end of the line and sits. The winner is the first one to be seated with the correct item in her hands.

Catch and Say
PH–28

On a chart, list vowels or consonants that your students have studied. Have students stand in a large circle with one child in the center. That child tosses a ball to a child in the outside circle as she calls out one of the letters on your chart. The child who catches the ball must say a word that begins with the letter or ends with it, or a word that contains the letter. Then she tosses the ball back to the student in the center, who tosses it to a different student and calls out another letter.

TIP

Help children to monitor their own understanding with these desk signs. Make "tents" with oak tag for children to keep at their desks. On one side write *Help Wanted* and on the other, *No Help Needed*. Students turn their cards to the appropriate side when they are working independently and you are circulating to give help.

Caught in a Web
PH–29

Have students sit in a large circle. Hold up a ball of yarn and say, "When I toss the yarn to the first person, I will say a letter. That person has to say a word which begins (or ends) with that letter." That child holds onto the end of the yarn, says another letter, and tosses the yarn ball to another student, who must say a word that begins with the new letter.

Use this activity to practice math facts, spin a story web, review vocabulary words, or to sequence events in a story or steps in a set of directions. You'll think of even more ways to use a yarn web.

❧ A to Z Word Pockets
PH-30 👁

Glue 26 library card pockets onto a large piece of poster board. Write a letter of the alphabet on each pocket and place blank index cards in each one. Encourage students to use the cards to write words they learn. They file their word cards in the pocket that has the same letter on it as the beginning letter of the words on their cards. When other children need help writing those words, they visit the board, think about how the word they are trying to write might begin, and look in the correct pocket to find the spelling they need. To give children practice in letter fluency, take all the cards out and mix them up. Use a sand timer to see how quickly they can match the index cards to the corresponding letter pockets.

ABC Line Up
PH-31 ✎

Distribute individual plastic or foam letters or letter cards to groups of students. On the count of three, children in each group line up in correct alphabetical order as quickly as possible. As they catch on, it's fine if a group gets *g, k, p, o,* and *s,* for example. They should still be able to sequence themselves correctly. Remind them to look at the class alphabet poster if they have trouble.

In the class, randomly hand out a letter to each student and see how long it takes the whole class to get in the correct alphabetical order on your count of three. Don't worry if you don't have 26 students; they can still get in ABC order with the letters they have. Time them, mix up the letters, and let them do it again to try to beat their time. Have them try to do this with no talking for a challenge.

Rug Reading
PH-32 ✎

Collect carpet-sample squares from a local flooring or furniture store and using 18-inch stencils, spray paint a letter of the alphabet on each one. Children use the carpets to walk the alphabet, skip over vowels, sit with friends on words they've assembled, and more.

Fluency

Fluent Me!
FL-1

With your students, discuss what fluent reading sounds like. Have them practice reading a story aloud a few times, and then let them use phonics phones (available through Crystal Springs Books) to read a passage or story into a tape recorder. Then have them play back the recording and follow along in their books as they listen to themselves read. You might design a simple rubric for them to use to rate themselves on their fluency. This could include whether they got stuck on any words, whether they paid attention to different kinds of punctuation, and whether they sounded like they were speaking. They might rate their performance on a scale from 1 to 5. Give students opportunities to retape their readings so they can improve their fluency each time.

Preread to Reread
FL-2

When a student needs to work on becoming more fluent, try this strategy. First, read the selection aloud for him (this is the prereading), and then have him read it back to you twice. The second time he reads, it is referred to as a "warm" read. Next do a vocabulary check. Review any words that your student stumbled on. After that, ask him three comprehension questions and finally have him do a "hot," or practiced, reread.

Fluency Boxes
FL-3 👁

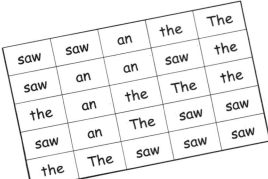

Using blank grids with five sections across and five sections down, create fluency boxes for any letters or words that a student is having trouble mastering. (See p. 175 for a blank grid you can use.) In random fashion, write three or four words repeatedly, one in each blank box. Give the student a fancy pointer or a mini pointer (available through Crystal Springs Books) and one minute to read as many words correctly as he can. Time him so he can compete against himself to increase accuracy and fluency.

You can also use this strategy for math fluency so that students become fluent at reading numbers, coins, fractions, decimals, and more. See page 195 for a coin fluency chart reproducible, for example. Some children have trouble reading numbers with three, four, and five digits, especially when one of the values is zero. They may read the number *7,802* as *seven thousand eighty-two*.

Sentence and Phrase Flash Cards
FL-4 👁

When a student needs to practice seeing and reading text in chunks instead of word by word, try this. Write phrases, such as *the big brown dog, in the house,* and *ran away fast,* or short sentences such as *I like cats* on separate flash cards. The student reads as many as she can in one minute. Keep track of her progress as she competes against herself and trains her eyes to read more than one word at a time.

Hear Me Grow
FL-5 👂

To demonstrate fluency development and build a student's confidence, tape record the student's reading every couple of weeks. Allow time for him to hear his previous taped reading sample before he records a new one. Discuss what he did well in his previous one and what he needs to work on with his new sample.

Impress Method
FL-6 🔊

In this strategy, a student reads aloud while you read aloud with him, but at a slightly faster rate. The student follows along with his pointer finger or a tracker (see p. 52). Continue for five minutes before asking any comprehension questions.

Fluency Flashlights
FL-7 👁

Purchase a few small, squeezable flashlights and try this bright idea. When a student needs to work on reading fluently, hold the flashlight for him and track along the page of text with it, holding it close enough to create a small ray of light. The student's eyes follow the light to read the text. The next time through the text, allow the student to hold the flashlight. Document his fluency each time by recording the number of words the student reads correctly and with fluency in one minute.

> **TIP**
>
> Have students read a paragraph or short story either silently or aloud, then ask them to try to tell you the main idea in one breath.

Nonsense Word Slapjack
FL-8 👁 ✋

For nonsense word fluency, play slapjack with a deck of nonsense words that use the CVC pattern. Write different nonsense words on index cards or blank playing

---

FLUENCY

Fluent readers can decode with few errors and can understand text quickly. They recognize most words and read them with automaticity. Fluent readers also see and read words in groups or chunks, instead of reading word by word. To become fluent, children need many opportunities to hear good readers reading aloud. They must be able to recognize most of the words they read so they don't have to stop to decode, and they need lots of practice reading aloud and rereading familiar text. When fluent readers read orally, they sound natural, as if they are speaking, and they read with good expression and comprehension.

cards. Include words such as *mip, pom, tup, rop, lup, kep, bap, bup, sut*, and so on. Choose one that you want children to focus on, for example, *lup*. Students turn over their cards one at a time and when a *lup* card appears, the first child to say it and slap it takes the whole pile. Children enjoy the nonsense words as well as the game, and they'll be practicing letter and sound fluency.

☙ Moving Picture Books
FL-9 👁

To encourage children to reread text for fluency, ask them to bring in several photos from home or use classroom photos. Glue these onto a long strip of oak tag. Fold a 12 x 18-inch paper in half, cut a hole out of the center, and cover the hole with clear acetate to resemble a TV screen. The picture frames should slide in and through the "window." Children can flip the pages and view their movies as they read photo captions they have written or dictated to an adult.

To focus on learning new words, have students use a vocabulary word from a literature or content area list in each caption. If your class takes a field trip as part of a unit of study, take along a camera or ask a chaperone to take pictures you can use for this activity. Students will use vocabulary connected with the unit when they write the sentences to accompany each photo.

Word Fluency Ladders
FL-10

When a student needs to read words with automaticity to become a fluent reader, try this strategy. Cut ladders out of oak tag and have the student write new sight words or vocabulary words, one on each rung, until her ladder is full. Have an adult or a buddy time her as she reads the words from the bottom of the ladder to the top. How quickly can she recognize and read the words? Students keep track of their progress and compete only with themselves for this strategy. When one ladder has been mastered, store it in a folder with the child's name on it so that she can review those words from time to time. Then start another ladder for the child with new words.

⚓ Sight-Word Cereal Books
FL-11 👁

Use empty cereal (and cracker) boxes that are familiar to children to make these books. Cut out the front panels, laminate them if you wish, and bind them together into a book with chicken rings or any other way. Watch children read them over and over again to practice becoming fluent readers!

> **TIP**
>
> Team a fluent reader with one who needs to work on this skill and have them practice reading familiar stories together. The student who is working on fluency will hear a student modeling the skill and will also be rereading familiar text, which is necessary practice for becoming fluent.

If your school cafeteria uses individual cereal boxes for school breakfasts, these make great little books that children can even take home and read to their parents. Tie the Sight-Word Cereal Books into the importance of eating a healthy breakfast or graphing how much sugar different cereals contain. Ask parents to send in the front panels to save yourself time and work.

Sight Word Snatch
FL-12 👁 🖐 ©

Write sight words on large cards and give each child a card, except for one child who is "it." Children hold up their cards. Call out a word and if the child without a card finds it within a time limit you set, she takes that card.

Trackers
FL-13 👁

Purchase plastic paws or fingers from a novelty shop (they're especially easy to find around Halloween). Children can place a paw or finger over their own finger to use for visual tracking. Squeeze flashlights and small pointers with stars and other shapes also work great, as well as "Bugle" chips, which fit over their fingers and can be eaten at the end of the lesson. (Remember to check for allergies if you use food.)

Word-Family Books
FL-14

Create books that students can read based on word families they recognize. A page might look like this:

> Tide
>
> I can read tide.
>
> Now . . .
>
> I can read ride.
>
> I can read wide.

Leave room for children to add more words to each page of their books. For example, on the page above, you would repeat the sentence stem, *I can read,* and insert a line for the student to add *side* and *hide.*

⚓ I Can Read
FL-15 👁

Students use pictures and words cut out of magazines and newspapers to create their own *I Can Read* books. Have each student choose eight or ten words he can read fluently. Glue each word and a matching picture, either cut out or drawn by the child, on a separate piece of paper. Bind the pages together into a book any way you like. Students can practice reading these by themselves, with a buddy, with an adult, or with their parents at home.

Fast, Faster, Fluent!
FL-16 👁

Create these sets of sight-word flash cards at different reading levels to use with individual students. Fold a piece of paper in half and have the student write her name and the date on it. Label one half of the paper *Fast* and the other half *Faster*. Hold up a flash card and have the student read it. If she reads the word or words on the card fluently, she gets a tally mark under *Faster*. If she stumbles over them, she gets a tally mark under *Fast*. The next time, have her record the date again and use a marker in a different color to make tally marks. This is a good way for students to measure their own progress.

⚓ Zipped-Up Sentences
FL-17 👁 🐾

On a strip of oak tag or an index card, write a complete sentence. Cut it into individual words (or phrases) and put the pieces in a resealable plastic bag. Have your student empty the bag and arrange the pieces to create a sentence. Use a timer to target fluency and automaticity.

> **TIP**
>
> Be careful that students don't confuse fluency with speed. Children who focus on reading with breakneck speed tend to lose comprehension in the process.

For content area study, write sentences that explain or describe vocabulary that students need to know. For example, you might write: *A habitat is a place where a living organism can get all its needs met.*

To make this a self-checking strategy, have a word written on the back of the strip before you cut it apart. For example, the sentence above on habitat might reveal the word *environment* when the pieces are arranged in the correct sequence and then flipped over.

More I Can Read
FL-18 👁

This activity reminds students of everything they have learned to read. It's a great way for a reluctant reader to measure progress and build confidence. Bind pages together into a book that demonstrates all the different ways a student can read and title it *More I Can Read.*

The first page might have color swatches but no words, showing that the child can "read" colors. The second page could have pictures of animals that the student can recognize instantly and name. The next page can show shapes that the child will recognize and name with instant recall, such as *circle*, *square*, and *triangle*. The fourth page may show a child going up and down steps with the words *up* and *down* with corresponding arrows for cueing on the page to show that she understands direction words. Include pictures to "read" such as "feelings faces" (happy, sad, angry, scared); weather symbols such as a sun, clouds, snow-flakes, and raindrops; the alphabet; numbers; and classmates' names. As the student becomes more confident and her skills increase, go back and add the words to the pictures on each page.

Blast Off!
FL-19 👁

Draw a rocket-ship launchpad with a different sight word written on each level. Mark the levels, starting at the bottom, 10, 9, 8, 7, and so on, marking the 0 as *Blast Off!* The child says each word with automaticity to see how far she can get. Use a timer to note progress and when a student recognizes the words instantly, start over with new words she needs to master.

Big and Little Readers
FL-20

Young children love to read with older students. Team up with a teacher whose students are two or three grades ahead of your class. Pair each older student with a younger one and have reading-buddy time at least every two weeks for 15 or 20 minutes. Older students read a book to younger ones and then younger students read to their older buddies. The older students should be reminded that they are role models for fluency for younger students, so they need to choose books they will be able to read aloud fluently. To keep all students from going off-task, set a time limit for buddy reading sessions.

Window Boxes
FL–21 👁

Use index cards to help students track words or to eliminate extra stimuli from their reading books. For younger children, a window or slit cut out of an index card works well. When you use a transparency on the overhead, use a large piece of oak tag with a box cut out to help learners focus on the part of the transparency that you are explaining or discussing.

And all the animals were happy in their new home. Then [monkey] ls all we new hotr nd all we new home all right in the morning time. Then we left for home.

Missing Words
FL–22 👁

Use this group activity to give students practice with instant recall. Write four sight words on the board. Students read the words and use them in sentences. Then the students cover their eyes and you erase one word. They uncover their eyes and try to guess which word is missing and use it in a sentence. The word is then put back on the board for self-checking. Add more words as students become more proficient at this task.

Readers' Theater
FL–23

Readers' theater scripts are great for building fluency. You can find free scripts for readers' theater on the Internet and in some teacher-resource books. Most children enjoy these and because they don't involve props, costumes, or memorizing lines, they aren't stressful for children and they don't require much prep time for teachers. Students build fluency by reading and rereading a script out loud. Some scripts involve choral readings that make it easier for shy students to take part. Have students rehearse with partners or in a small group, so they get more opportunities to reread for fluency.

Bingo
FL–24 👁 ✎

On a set of index cards or blank flash cards, glue a picture of a sight word such as a ball, a cake, a truck, or a car on one side of each card. Write the word on the other side. Make grid boards similar to bingo boards with each sight word

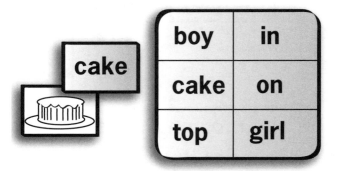

written on them in a different box on each board and give one to each child. Cards are placed with the word side up in a pile. The child must be able to say the word correctly before placing it on the matching word on his board. The picture on the back makes the game self-correcting.

Use the same format for rhyming words, initial sounds, and letter matching.

Three-Star Rings
FL–25 👁

Give students silver notebook rings. Write words they need to review for instant recall on index cards and punch a hole in each card and slip it onto the ring. A star sticker is placed on the upper left-hand corner of a card each time the student reads the word with automaticity, or you can simply draw a star with a marker. When a student's card has three stars, it is removed from the ring and another card is added. File the cards that you remove in a folder or envelope so that the child can review them later. Some teachers ask parents to send in small recipe-file boxes that students then decorate and use for their cards.

Let's All Show
FL–26

Pass out identical packs of sight words on flash cards to students in small groups or the whole class. Have the children arrange their cards face up on their desks. Call out a word that the children have in their deck, count to three to give students a few seconds to locate the card, and say, "Let's all show." Students hold the card against their foreheads so you can see it. This gives you a quick assessment of who needs more practice with particular sight words.

Tape Talk
FL–27 🔊

For this strategy, a teacher or volunteer records a list of ten sight words on a tape. The words are also written on a sheet of paper, along with sentences using each word. The student follows along and points to the words as he hears them read. Immediately after this follow-and-point activity, the tape gives the words in context and the child points to each word in a sentence. Next, the tape says a word and gives the listener a specific direction involving that word. For example, the child might hear, "Find the word *talk* on the list. Put a triangle over the word *talk*. Now find *boy*. Draw two lines under the word *boy*." Use a timer to track a child's progress in fluency.

Poetic Justice
FL–28 👁 🖐 🔊

Each month, choose four short poems and type them on squared-off index cards. Laminate these and attach one poem to each side of a cardboard cube, such as the boxes that gift coffee mugs come in, or make cubes using the pattern on page 171. The children sit in a circle and take turns rolling the cube. Each one reads or recites, alone or with a partner, whichever poem lands on top. If you send the poems home with students so they can rehearse, most students will feel comfortable reciting them in class.

LANGUAGE MASTER ACTIVITIES

The Language Master has been around for many years, but this device is still popular with children and useful for teachers. Language Masters are often referred to as mid-level assistive technology aids. They are recording devices that allow teachers to write a word on a card, dictate the word, and have it available for the student to use. Students work independently with the Language Master. They slide a card through the device to see the word, hear it, say it, and then define it. Cards are about 3 x 8 inches with a recordable strip across the bottom and are big enough to add corresponding visual cues such as words or pictures.

Teachers can also record multistep directions on the cards, one step per card. Students who have trouble remembering directions can hear one direction or all of the steps again.

For a reading comprehension activity, label the sides of the cube *who, what, where, when, why,* and *how.* Students roll the cube to answer the question that lands on top about a book the class is reading.

For younger students, write a different word-family word on each side of the cube. Now when students roll the cube, they must name a word that rhymes with the word on the top.

Songs and Rhymes
FL–29 ◖◗

Children enjoy silly songs, chants, and jump-rope rhymes and can usually repeat them fluently. Capitalize on the skill by using Miss Mary Mack, Tony Chestnut, My Aunt Came Back, and other old favorites as fluency warm-ups. Remind children to try to use the same fluent voices when they read.

Vocabulary

CATegories
VO–1 👁

Write a list of sight words or vocabulary words on a large paper cutout of a cat. (See the reproducible pattern on p. 176.) Write the appropriate category for the words on the cat's tail and put the cat in a brown paper bag. For example, if your students are reviewing a science unit and the words include *mammal*, *reptile*, and *amphibian*, the category you write on the cat's tail might be *kinds of animals*. Tell the students that you will slowly let the cat out of the bag. They must read the words on the cat as each one appears and try to figure out what the category is before the cat is let all the way out of the bag. Categories could also be sight words, CVC words, nonsense words, or other words connected to a content area, such as words that name geometric shapes or words that have to do with a unit on oceans.

dog
sheep
cat
horse
lion

animals

🐾 Find It, Define It
VO–2 👁

Give each student a sheet of paper with a box drawn on it for each new vocabulary word he needs to learn. Write the new word and the page in the reading book where the student will find it. Have the students illustrate their words, using color to enhance memory. Then have them add a definition or word description in their own words and a synonym for the new word.

Compound Concentration
VO-3 🗞 👁

List 20 different compound words on a sheet of paper. Next, write each part of the compound word on a separate index card. For example, if you have written the compound word *rainbow* on your list, you will write *rain* on one index card and *bow* on another one. Place the forty index cards face down in a 5 by 8 grid with eight cards in a row and five rows. A student turns over two cards. If the words on the cards can be put together to form a compound word that is on your list, the student keeps the two cards. If the two words cannot be joined to form a compound word, they are returned to their places face down and the next student takes a turn. You can do this with vocabulary words and definitions, too.

Word Chains
VO-4 👁

On a sheet of blank paper, draw 5 to 8 loops large enough for children to write in, or use the reproducible on page 178. Write a number 1 or draw a star in one of the loops and give the paper to one child in a small group of students. That child writes a word in the starred or numbered loop and hands the paper to the next child, who must write a word in the second loop that is related to the first word, and so on until all of the loops are filled. The last word written must also connect in some way to the first word written and to the other words as well.

VOCABULARY

Vocabulary is the ability to understand receptive language and use expressive language to make oneself understood. To comprehend text, readers must know what most of the words mean. If they have to slow down to decode unfamiliar words frequently, meaning is lost. Vocabulary includes listening vocabulary that children must know to understand what they hear, speaking vocabulary, reading vocabulary, and writing vocabulary.

Children learn many words indirectly when they listen to a story, engage in conversation, and read on their own. But they need explicit instruction in how to recognize context clues and how to use them to figure out word meanings. In addition, they need explicit instruction to learn not only content area words and academic language but also strategies for learning and understanding new words.

For example, if the first loop has the word *whale* written in it, subsequent loops might say *mammal, large, baleen, toothed, migrates*, and so on.

This strategy also works well for character studies. The first child writes the name of a character in the first loop and other children write words or phrases to describe the way that the character looks or acts or things he does in the book. You can also use it for synonyms. Younger students can work on letter sequence; the first student may write *J* and the next would write *K*.

For content area studies, students write words that are connected to the unit. For structural analysis, give students sheets with a root word already written in the first loop. They pass it around the group and each one tries to record a different word that uses the same root. If the root word in the first loop is *cook*, children might write the words *cooked, cooking, uncooked, precook*, and *cookbook*.

⚓ Riddle Writers
VO-5

Have students write riddles for each of the words in their vocabulary list. Place the riddles in a jar or a folder. Students can pair off and take turns reading the riddles and guessing the words. Some examples of riddles you can show students to get them started might include the following:

> I am a vocabulary word with 6 letters.
>
> I am the vocabulary word that has one *m* and two *t*'s.
>
> I am the word _____.

Fast Match
VO-6 👁

To help students recognize words automatically, make two sets of cards in two different colors, one color with pictures of sight words and the other color with the corresponding words. Spread the cards face down. One student chooses two cards, one of each color, and looks at them. He reads the word. If the picture card and the word card match, he keeps them and the next student takes a turn. The student with the most matches at the end of the game wins.

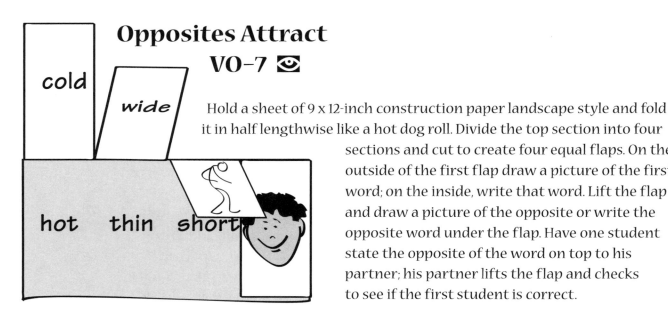

Opposites Attract
VO-7 👁

Hold a sheet of 9 x 12-inch construction paper landscape style and fold it in half lengthwise like a hot dog roll. Divide the top section into four sections and cut to create four equal flaps. On the outside of the first flap draw a picture of the first word; on the inside, write that word. Lift the flap and draw a picture of the opposite or write the opposite word under the flap. Have one student state the opposite of the word on top to his partner; his partner lifts the flap and checks to see if the first student is correct.

⚓ Sticker Spelling
VO-8 ✋ 👁

Purchase sets of letter stickers at office supply stores or discount stores and give each student a page of letters. Students use the stickers for spelling or vocabulary tests rather than writing the words with pencil and paper.

Sight Word Bean-O
VO-9 ✋

Use dried lima beans for this activity. Write a sight word for review on each bean with a fine-tipped, permanent marker. Place five to ten beans in an empty film container.

Divide the students into pairs. Have one student shake his container of beans out onto the table. The other team member must read each word, define it, and use it in a sentence.

This activity also lends itself to individualized review. Create a different container for each student according to the words she needs to review, place a label on it, and write her name on the label. When she has mastered the words, put new words in the film container for her to practice.

Sight Word Slapjack
VO-10 ■

Use a set of index cards or blank flash cards for this game. Write each word or sentence to be reviewed on two cards. For example, if a word to be reviewed is *rhombus*, you will write that word on two cards. Shuffle the cards and deal them out equally to two students. Students play the game slapjack, each turning over one card at the same time. When two identical words are laid on the table face up, the first child to call out that word or sentence wins the entire pile.

Program your blank cards with nonsense words and direct students to play the same way. This is a fun way for them to practice sounding out phonemes, too.

⚓ Sight Word Tie-Ups
VO-11 👁 ■

Draw or glue a picture representing the sight word or vocabulary word you want to review in the center of a 4 x 6-inch index card. In each corner of the card, write a different word, one of which correctly identifies the picture. Students stretch a piece of yarn (an 8-inch piece works fine) from the picture in the center to the correct word in one of the corners. On the back of the card, draw a line showing the position of the picture in relation to the correct word, so students can check their work for instant feedback.

This strategy can be adapted for math problems and comprehension questions.

Unscrambled List
VO-12

Give struggling spellers a list of spelling words with the first letters missing. Have them add the initial letters to spell the words correctly. Time them to increase automaticity.

Good spellers enjoy having all the letters in the words scrambled and being timed. The same activity can be used for vocabulary and sight words.

⚓ Timely Definitions
VO-13 👁

Invite students to write a year 2008 definition for a sight or a vocabulary word, and then an 1860 definition for the same word. For example, students in 2008 might define *web* as a worldwide information superhighway, but in 1860, the definition for the word *web* would have been what spiders build in the barn. Let students illustrate and add color to their definitions for added learning.

Sticky-Note Spelling
VO-14 📇

Using the smallest sticky notes available, write one letter on each note for each letter in the student's spelling words. Give a spelling test and allow the student to spell his words using the stickies.

Strong Words
VO-15 👂

Challenge students to be specific about words they use in their speech and writing with questions such as:

> Which word is stronger—big or enormous?
>
> Which word is scarier—spooky or terrifying?
>
> Which word is better—pretty or gorgeous?
>
> Which word smells worse—odor or scent?
>
> Which word is tastier—delicious or scrumptious?

Later, have them generate their own questions using vocabulary they've learned from their reading. They'll have to work with synonyms to do this, so have dictionaries and thesauruses on hand at the various reading levels your students need. Have them drop their questions in a box or fishbowl and you can pull them out when there are a few minutes to spare. Students must tell you why they prefer one word over another.

Magic Fly Swatter
VO-16 ▨ ◉

Get a plastic fly swatter from a dollar store or a Word Whacker (available from Crystal Springs Books) and cut out a window. Use it to "grab" vocabulary words off transparencies when you're using the overhead and to target specific words on charts or in big books and pull them in and out of context. Let students use them to target words they are unsure of.

All the ani███ ██ smiling and happy. An█ ████ ██ey all jumped for joy beca███ ██ said it was time to leave ██ ██e coast. The elephants wal█ed to the boat, the kangaroos am█led over to say their farewells █nd the sunset cast a red glo█ over the group.

⚓ Reading and Writing the Room
VO-17 ▨ ◉

Children love to read and write the room. Take a sheet of paper and fold it to make four boxes. Label each box with an element you want children to review. Then make copies for students, have clipboards available, and let them go. You might include directions such as the following:

- Find and write six compound words.
- Find and copy five words with short vowel sounds in the middle.
- Find and write four words that have three syllables each.
- Find and copy three words that begin with capital letters because they name a special person, place, or thing.

Ticket Spelling
VO-18 ▨ ◧

Give each student three to five carnival or raffle tickets (or use the reproducible on p. 179) to use in this fun vocabulary or spelling review. Appoint one student as the caller. The student calls out a word; other students who think they can define the word or spell it hold a ticket in front of their mouths. The caller chooses one of them to define or spell the word; if the student is correct, she writes her name on the ticket and places it in a hat or fishbowl. She then becomes the caller. When she has called out a new word and chosen another student to define or spell it, if the student is right, he writes his name on one of his tickets, drops it in the hat, and takes her place. She returns to her seat and rejoins the play. When all words have been reviewed, a ticket is drawn from the fishbowl, and the student whose name is drawn wins a prize, such as a "no homework" coupon, an oral (as opposed to written) spelling test, or fifteen minutes with a favorite computer program. Choose three names to make it even more exciting.

Scrambled Eggs
VO-19 👁 🐾

Write each letter of the student's spelling words, sight words, or vocabulary words separately on a paper egg. Scramble the eggs and have the student unscramble them by spelling each word with the paper eggs. This is also a good strategy for students who have trouble writing words for a spelling test. Use a timer to encourage fluency.

⚓ Vocabulary Journals
VO-20 👁

Have students keep individual journals where they record at least two new words they learn every day. Have them include the date, definitions, and illustrations for each one. You might also want them to write each one in a sentence. Occasionally, review journals as a prewriting activity and remind students to try to use these words in any kind of writing they do. You might also want to keep a class vocabulary journal and add to it daily or appoint a different student to do this each week. Students who have been absent can copy words and definitions they've missed.

⚓ Wacky Words
VO-21 👁

Invite students to come up with the silliest sentences they can think of using new vocabulary words correctly, and then write and illustrate their sentences. For example, if *nagging* is one of their new words from a story, they might write *Mrs. Goodman keeps nagging the principal to put a Starbucks in the teacher's room.* Allow them to share their sentences with a buddy or with the class. If you have students write and illustrate their sentences on separate sheets of paper, you can bind these together and place them in the classroom library to be read again and again.

Close Shave Quizzes
VO-22 🔧

Once in a while, have a shaving cream spelling test. Squirt a golf-ball sized dollop of unscented shaving cream on the student's desk. Have him write each spelling word in the shaving cream. Remind students to keep their soapy hands away from their face and eyes. (This is also a great way to clean desks before vacation or after a party.)

Tapping Teammates
VO-23 🔄

Have the children stand in a line and appoint one child to be the teacher's assistant. Give your assistant a spelling word on an index card. She reads the word aloud, then taps another child on the shoulder. The second child must say the first letter in the word and wait for a nod of approval from the assistant. If he is correct, he then taps the next child, who must give the second letter of the word. The children continue until they spell the word correctly.

TIP

Try this strategy for students who have trouble with organization. Get some 8 x 10-inch manila envelopes and remove the brass brads. Laminate them, then slit them open. On the front of the envelope, write the cues the student needs. He checks off each one just like we do for the Internal Revenue Service. These make good homework organizers, too. Allow the student to answer the questions with a wipe-off crayon or marker. For example, you might write the following:

1. Did you remember to write your name on your work? Yes No

2. Did you write today's date on your work? Yes No

3. Have you checked to see if you completed the assignment? Yes No

When you can circle every *yes*, please place your envelope in the all-done basket.

ꙮ Shake and Spell
VO-24 ▨

With a fine-point permanent marker, write letters on one side of individual bingo chips. Make sure you have enough of each letter to spell all the words in the current word or spelling list. Place the bingo chips in a coffee can or other container. Give children the list of words you want them to practice and have them shake the chips out of the can and spell the words.

Twirl-a-Word
VO-25 ▨

Give each student a slender dowel about 16 inches long to which you have attached a shiny piece of ribbon about eight inches long. (If you cap one end of the dowel with a pencil-top eraser, you can pin the ribbon to it.) Let them practice spelling and vocabulary words in the air. Make sure they stand at least a yard apart from each other so no one gets poked. They should say the word before they start to twirl, say each letter as they twirl it, and then repeat the word when they are done. Ask students to give you the definition for each word before going on to the next.

A variation of this is to use flashlights on a chalkboard. Use squeezable or other small flashlights, put the lights off, and let students practice their words by flashing their lights onto the chalkboard.

Words on a Walk
VO-26 ▨

On index cards, write the vocabulary words that you want students to review. Then give students headbands or sweatbands to put on. Slip a word card into the front of each child's headband. On your signal, the students and their words go walking around the room. Students ask each other for clues as they try to guess what word you have placed in their headband. Encourage them to ask questions that can only be answered with *yes* or *no*. For example, if students have been studying rocks and minerals, vocabulary words might include *metamorphic*, *sedimentary*, *lava*, *igneous*, and *erosion*. Questions they ask each other could include "Am I a type of rock?" and "Do I come from a volcano?"

⚓ Climbing Up the Alphabet
VO-27 👁

Create a large cutout of a staircase with 13 steps. Write two letters on the top of each step in alphabetical order—AB, CD, EF, etc.—until you've written the whole alphabet on the steps. On the vertical part of each step, have a child write two words beginning with the two letters on the step. Make sure the student writes the words in alphabetical order.

If you make this as a large poster and laminate it, children can reuse it as an anchor activity. Older students might be asked to use vocabulary words from a current unit of study, such as *B-biomes, C-carnivore,* and so on. Tell students they can incorporate the *x* into a word instead of starting a word with it.

30-Second Word Storm
VO-28

To activate prior knowledge before you introduce a new book or unit of study, ask students to list as many words related to the topic as they can in 30 seconds. For example, if you are going to be teaching a unit on geology, ask them to list as many ways to describe rocks as they can in 30 seconds. If you are studying geography, they might list as many states as they can in 30 seconds. When you repeat this exercise during a unit and after, you should see their lists growing longer. Be sure to ask students to share their lists with a buddy or small group, and then with the whole class. This helps students who had a word "on the tip of their tongue" to hear it. If possible, team up good writers with those who have trouble encoding or physically writing words quickly so that these students have their words included.

To use 30-Second Word Storm with literature, tell your students the setting or a little bit about the book. For example, if they will be reading Roald Dahl's *The BFG*, you might ask them to list words related to giants, England, orphanages, and so on.

⚓ Word Target
VO-29 👁

Give students a list of vocabulary words that they need to know from a content area or from their reading. As they look at the list, ask questions such as:

Find a word that means the same as _____.

Find a word that means the opposite of _____.

Find a word that is an example of _____.

Find a word that has the same root (or affix) as _____.

To use this strategy with younger students, ask questions such as:

Find a word with a silent letter.

Which word on this list has the most syllables?

Is there a compound word on this list?

Which word on this list rhymes with _____?

If you write your questions, students can do this as an anchor activity and record their responses so that you can check them later.

Prefix or Suffix Bingo
VO-30 📷

Write a prefix or suffix on each side of a cube made from a coffee mug box or use cubes purchased at a craft store. (You can also make your own using the pattern on p. 171.) Make bingo cards containing 19 root words and a free space. Appoint one student to roll the cube and call out the prefix or suffix that lands on top. Keep a list of the affixes that are called on the board so they can be checked when a student calls Bingo. If a student has a root word on her card that can be joined to the prefix or suffix that was called to make a real word, she covers the root word with a bingo chip. The first child to cover a row shouts, "Bingo!" but must tell you her words before she is declared the winner and becomes the new caller.

For this game, tell students not to worry about root word spellings that would need to change, but do write them on the board or mention them in the course of play. For example, if a student has the root word *hike* and the caller calls out the suffix *ing*, the student will cover the root word *hike* because *hiking* is a real word. You would just want to mention that the letter *e* on *hike* would be dropped before the *ing* was added if you were writing the new word.

⚓ Here's the Scoop
VO-31 🔧

Using colored construction paper or oak tag, create ice cream cones and scoops of ice cream. Have students sort cones and scoops to practice matching vowel sounds to words, combining words to create compound words, matching words to definitions, and more.

Laminate the pieces before you write on them so you can wipe off writing and reprogram them for a variety of activities.

You can also give students blank cones and scoops that have not been laminated. Have them write a character's name on the cone and a descriptive word on each scoop or a vocabulary word on the cone with synonyms on each scoop. They arrange their cones and scoops and then glue them onto a large sheet of construction paper.

TIP

For kinesthetic learners, play a game of "Vocabarades" using new vocabulary words. Play like charades. A student chooses a word from a hat and must act it out within a time limit you set. The student who guesses his word takes the next turn. Model for students how to show the number of syllables in a word and how to indicate a rhyming word.

Around the World
VO-32 🔧

Children love to play Around the World. Arrange chairs in a circle and have each child sit in a chair except for one student who tries to make it "around the world." Flash vocabulary words or sight words that you've written on cards. The first of the two students, one seated and one standing, to say the word correctly continues around the circle. The other student remains in or takes the seat.

This activity is excellent for reviewing math facts, too.

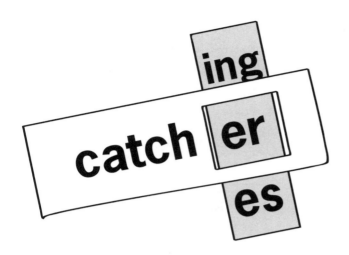

Super Suffixes
VO-33 👁 ✎

Cut a large piece of oak tag into 3 x 9-inch strips. Cut a 2 x 2-inch window in the right side of each strip. Write a base word on the left side of each strip, and a list of matching suffixes on a 2 x 6-inch piece of paper. Have a student read the base word on the strip along with each of the suffixes on the list to create new words. Use a sand timer to improve fluency.

Artful Vocabulary
VO-34 👁

Have the students use colored markers, crayons, calligraphy markers, or glitter pens for vocabulary practice. Color enhances their ability to recall words and their meanings. Use large unlined index cards or half-sheets of white construction paper for the words. The brighter and crazier they make the letters in each word, the better. Have each child choose his best work to frame with a construction paper border. Display these on a bulletin board in the classroom or in the hall. Have an art show!

Vocabulary Links
VO-35 👁 👂

Write vocabulary words from your students' reading or from a unit of study on index cards or pieces of oak tag drawn to resemble links in a chain. Spread the cards or links out on a table or attach them to the bulletin board. (Make sure every student can see all of the cards.) Call on one student to choose a word and use it in a sentence. The next student chooses another card and uses that word in a sentence to build onto the first student's sentence. For example, if your students are studying the solar system, their "links" might include *rotation, revolve, gravity,* and *planets.* Student A might choose *rotation* and use a sentence such as *Rotation is when something stays in one place but spins around.* Student B might choose the word *planets* and use the sentence *The planet we live on has rotation and that gives us day and night.*

Guess and Flip
VO-36

Write the letters of a vocabulary word that students need to know on individual sheets of construction paper, one letter per sheet. Tape the sheets of paper, blank side up, onto the chalkboard or marker board. Give the students a definition of the word. Then have them take turns guessing which letters are in the word. As a student guesses a letter correctly, flip the paper so that the letter is visible. That student continues to guess letters until she guesses incorrectly. The student who guesses what the word is may put up the next word.

Suspicious Vocabulary
VO-37 [icon]

Have the students work in pairs for this activity based on the game Suspicion. Each pair has a stack of cards with vocabulary words written on them. Partners don't see each other's words. The first student chooses a card from his stack and gives the definition for the suspicious word to his partner, who must state what the word is. If his partner is correct, then it's her turn to choose a card from her stack and define it. If the first student is right, he is cleared of suspicion and now becomes the detective, choosing the card, defining the word, and checking his partner's answer.

> **TIP**
>
> Provide students with a list of new sight words at a learning center and a variety of sensory ways to review the words. As a child reviews each word on the list, he writes the word with three different kinds of materials. He could write each word with glitter glue, Play-Doh, on sandpaper, with Wikki Stix, or in a shoe box filled with salt. Tactile learners especially benefit from these activities.

Antonym, Synonym, or Homonym Match
VO-38 [icon]

Use two sets of cards in two colors for this game. If you are having students work on antonyms and your cards are green and blue, for example, you might write *quiet* on a green card and *noisy* on a blue card. Mix up the cards and place them face down in a grid pattern. Children take turns choosing two cards. If they match words that are antonyms, such as *quiet* and *noisy*, they keep the pair. If not, they put them back and the next child chooses. Whoever has the most cards at the end of the game or when time is up is the winner.

Antonym or Synonym Bingo
VO-39 🖑 👁

Distribute blank bingo cards to each student. Create a set of index cards with all the words you want to review. Before the game, review these words with the students and have them write a synonym or antonym for each word in a spot on the bingo cards. Collect and redistribute the cards and begin the bingo game. Use the index cards to call words, but remind students that they are looking for either an antonym or a synonym for the word you call. You might introduce this game using only synonyms or antonyms so that students get the hang of it before you use both in one game.

Group Tic-Tac-Toe
VO-40 🖑

Create and laminate a large tic-tac-toe grid on poster board. Write a vocabulary word or a sight word in each section. Divide students into two teams. Give a definition for one of the words, then give each team a chance to identify the word. A player from team one comes to the grid and puts an *X* on the word he thinks matches the definition. If he is right, leave the *X*. If not, erase it and give team two a chance to mark the word that matches your definition. (Team two writes an *O*.) The next definition goes first to team two. The first team to get three marks in a row wins the round.

Using Context Clues to Solve a Mystery
VO-41 👁

Write each vocabulary word on an index card and place the cards in an envelope. On a separate piece of paper, write a sentence that contains a context clue for each one of the words in the envelope. Leave a blank in each sentence where the missing word would go. Number the sentences. Have the students use the context clues provided by the sentences to match the index cards to the correct sentences. Mark the corresponding sentence number on the back of each index card so students can check their own answers.

⚓ Analogy a Day
VO-42

Analogies are great vocabulary builders, and most children enjoy analogies once they get the hang of them. Start with simple ones that use opposites, such as *hot* is to *cold* as *short* is to *tall*. Leave out *short* or *tall* and let students discuss the possible answers with each other before you call on a student. When they understand analogies, students can work on them as an anchor activity. Incorporate words and concepts from units of study to make this strategy even more useful.

Teach students that sometimes there is more than one answer to an analogy, as in the example *neck* is to *necklace* as *wrist* is to *bracelet* or *wristwatch*. Once students understand how analogies work, teach them to use the single colon, double colon, single colon format (pencil : paper :: chalk : chalkboard). Students love shortcuts.

Snowball Fight
VO-43 ▪

Give each student a piece of scrap paper or a 9-inch square piece of white paper, and a list of vocabulary words for review. Have each student write a vocabulary word on her scrap paper, then crumple it up. At your signal, all students toss their snowballs, making absolutely sure that they aim below the shoulder. (If students are too aggressive, have them toss a snowball under another student's chair instead of throwing them at each other.) Let them toss snowballs back and forth for no longer than 10 seconds. When you say stop, each student opens up the "snowball" in her hand or picks one up from the floor if she doesn't happen to be holding one. She tells the class what word she has on her paper and gives a definition for it. She may ask for help if she does not know the meaning.

Use this strategy with comprehension questions from literature and with questions from a content area unit, too.

TIP

Visual learners enjoy creating nonlinguistic representations of words, such as symbols or rebuses for new words. Have lots of markers with fine tips, wide tips, and even calligraphy tips available for these learners. Remind them to use a lot of color in their illustrations to enhance memory.

Chillin' with Vocabulary
VO-44 ◤

Try this *chilling* approach to new vocabulary words. Cut five to ten ice cube shapes out of oak tag and laminate them. On each cube, use a vis-à-vis marker or wipe-off crayon to write a vocabulary word. Have the students sit in a circle. Start passing an ice cube around the circle while you play a winter song like "Frosty the Snowman" on the tape player. (This is especially fun in early fall and late spring when days can be very warm.) Stop the music suddenly. Whoever is holding the cube must read the word aloud, define it, and use it in a sentence. If the student needs assistance, he may ask for help from the student sitting to his left or right. If the student gives the correct answer, that cube is set aside and another cube is started around the circle.

6						
5						
4						
3						
2						
1						
	will	as	can	an	did	said

❧ Vocabulary Graphing
VO-45 ◉

Have students graph the frequency of target words in a passage or page of text. Use the reproducible on page 189 to create a word graph for the student. Write the words that you want your students to focus on along the bottom of a graph (the horizontal axis). As students read the assigned pages, they make a check mark every time a target word appears. This is good for sight word identification as well as for content area vocabulary.

Oh Say, Can You Say?
VO-46 ◖◗

Divide the class into pairs to review and reinforce vocabulary words. Give one student a word card. She must define and describe the word to her partner without saying what the word is. For example, she might say, "It's a large dinosaur and it flies. It is a meat eater and it is called a _____." Her partner must guess the word. Then they switch roles.

Whistle Stop
VO-47

Create two identical sets of vocabulary flash cards. Appoint one student to be the conductor, complete with a conductor's cap if you have one or a train whistle from Crystal Springs Books. Give the conductor one set of cards and distribute the other set to the students playing the game. The group sings a "choo-choo" chant, moving their arms to the chant. The conductor holds up one of her word cards and announces "Whistle stop!" The students stop their choo-choo chant, and the student with the card that matches the conductor's card says the word and uses it in a sentence. If the student is correct, he hands the card to the conductor. The group continues to play until all the cards are handed over to the conductor.

To use this game to review math facts, make two sets of cards, but write numbers from 1 to 20 on one set and corresponding addition or subtraction problems on the second set. The conductor holds up a number, which the train passengers must match to a corresponding fact card.

Alphabeta-Brainstorm
VO-48

To activate background knowledge before you begin a new unit, try this strategy. Determine a list of topics related to the unit. If you'll be studying rain forests, for example, one topic might be animals, another might be plants, and a third might be products from the rain forest. If you use animals as a topic, you can further divide it into mammals, birds, and reptiles, depending on the readiness level of your class. Divide the class into groups and give each group a different letter of the alphabet. The group that gets *B*, for instance, has 2 minutes to write down all the animals they think live in a rain forest and have names that start with *b*. Have the groups share their lists when time is up and let them add to their lists any words they heard during sharing. Then give the groups another topic such as plants, and assign a different letter to each group. Simplify this activity by letting groups list any words that fit the topic, regardless of the letter they start with.

What a Cover-up!
VO–49

Before students read an assigned chapter or selection, write each new vocabulary word from the text on a 5 x 8-inch index card. Distribute the cards to students and have them write or illustrate the definitions. Place the vocabulary cards on the floor with the words face down and the definitions showing. As the teacher calls out a word, the student covers the definition with her foot. If you are working at a table with a group of students, have them use their hand to cover the definition. This strategy works well for reinforcing and reviewing content area vocabulary.

Word Detective
VO–50

Write definitions for new vocabulary words from reading, math, or another content area on index cards and hide the cards around the room. On another set of index cards, write the matching vocabulary words. One student who is "it" wears a detective hat or badge and carries a magnifying lens to search the room for the definition to a word you give him written on a card. Set a time limit to make it more fun. When the detective makes a match, he takes the definition card and returns to his seat.

WORD MAGIC

Designate a special hat the magician's hat—you may be able to find a cardboard top hat at a craft or costume store. Write new words on small cards and drop them into the hat. When there's a minute or two to spare, let students choose one and tell you the meaning or use it in a sentence.

You can also invite your students to write new words they come across in their independent reading for this activity. Give each student a few blank cards and ask them to write any interesting words they meet as they are reading independently. If they don't know the meaning or cannot use the word in a sentence, give them a brief explanation. Because they write the word, they may remember it later when they see it again. You might want to have them record the title of the book and page number where they found the word, in case other students want to see how the word is used in context.

Pop-up Lollipops
VO-51

Write sight words or vocabulary words on lollipop heads cut out of construction paper and attach them to Popsicle sticks. On the lower portion of each Popsicle stick, draw a picture to match the word using a fine-point marker. Put the lollipops in a can with only the words showing. As a student reads the word, she picks the lollipop out of the can and checks the picture to see if she was right. If she read the word correctly, she keeps the lollipop. If not, she returns it to the can and the next student takes a turn.

Use the same idea for math facts. Write the problems on the lollipops and the answers on the sticks. You can also adapt this for initial or final consonant sounds by putting a picture on the top and the corresponding beginning (or final) letter on the stick. Another variation is to write a word on top or with younger students, use stickers that show a single object and place one sticker on each lollipop head. Ask the student to tell you how many phonemes are in the word, and then have her check by looking at the number on the stick.

Are You?
VO-52

Prepare a set of index cards with a vocabulary word, a sight word, or a spelling word written on each card. Tell the students that you are going to play a detective game. Have a child pick one of the cards. Make sure he doesn't let the others see what word is on his card. The other students must ask a variety of questions about the word that can be answered with *yes* or *no*; for example:

- Does your word have more than five letters?
- Is your word a verb?
- Does your word have an -*ing* ending?

The first student to successfully identify the vocabulary word chooses another card and answers questions from her classmates. Continue the game until all of the words have been described. If there's time, have students classify the words to reinforce learning. They might classify them according to number of syllables, number of letters, parts of speech, and so on.

❧ Pocket Folder Words
VO-53

Give students pocket folders and have them write their names on the front. On the left-hand pocket, they write *Words I Am Learning* and on the right-hand pocket they write *Words I Know*. Individual word cards are then transferred from one side to another as the student masters each one. Students pull these out to practice when they have a few minutes or work with a partner to quiz each other.

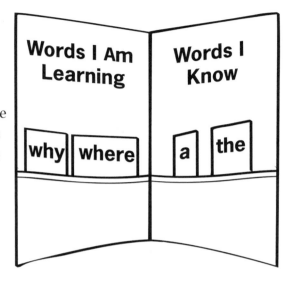

Inside-Outside Vocabulary Circles
VO-54

Have children form two circles, one inside another. Give the children in the outside circle cards with words written on them that students are learning. The children in the inside circle turn to face those in the outside circle. Inside-circle children must define the word written on the card that the person facing them is holding. Then direct the outside circle to move two children to the left. As the circle on the outside moves, inside-circle children give definitions for new words. When they return to their original positions, children switch places so the inside-circle children are now in the outside circle with the word cards and the children who were on the outside must now give the meanings of the words on the cards.

Missing Something?
VO-55

You'll need the same number of index cards for this activity as there are students in your room or in your group. If you have an uneven number of students, count yourself as a player. Divide the set of cards in half and write words to learn on half of the cards and their meanings on the other half. Hand out the cards randomly, and on your signal, students must find their partners. To make this more challenging, tell them they can't speak during the process. When a student with a word and a student with the matching definition have found each other, they sit down. (You might want them to create a sentence together using the word or illustrate it so that they are still engaged in the task while they wait for other students to find their matches.)

Context Detectives
VO-56 👁

To help students understand how to use context clues to figure out a word's meaning, try this strategy. Find 10 to 15 words in the dictionary that your students do not know. Write each of the words and its definition on an index card. Have the children work in groups. The first team member studies the word and its definition and then writes one or two sentences that use the word in context on a separate sheet of paper. The paper with the context clue is passed to the next member. If that member is able to define the word by using context clues only, the team receives a point.

TIP

Ask parents to write a note to their child and put it in his lunch or snack at least once a week. Keep a stack of blanks handy in case a student's parent is not able to take part in this. Have an aide write a note to the child or write one yourself. Provide parents with a sample set of notes. Send the week's vocabulary, spelling, or sight words home to parents and ask them to use some of the words in their notes.

Flip and Define
VO-57 🖐

Write vocabulary words on an inexpensive shower liner or plastic tablecloth. Students toss a penny onto it and must define the word their coin lands on or comes closest to. If they are correct, they take another turn. If they don't know the meaning of the word, they ask for help. Kinesthetic learners love to do this with sight words, too.

To use this strategy with number facts, program the plastic sheet with numbers. Students toss their penny and give a fact family for the number they land on. For example, if the penny lands on 7, the student may say 4 + 3.

✒ Flip-a-Root Charts
VO–58 👁 🖐

To reinforce prefixes or suffixes, use a white 5 x 8-inch index card and write the prefix or suffix on the right-hand side of the card (for suffixes) or on the left-hand side (for prefixes). Using different colored 3 x 5-inch cards, write a root word on each one. Hook the two sets of cards together at the top with word rings or a spiral binder. Have students flip the root words to make new words. Then have them say or write the definitions or use the new words they form in sentences.

Vocab-a-Scrabble
VO–59 🖐

Place old scrabble letters or individual letter squares in a container. Make sure the container is opaque so that the children cannot see the letters. Write each vocabulary word to be reviewed on individual sentence strips. Give each child a sentence strip. The child must pull one letter from the container. If he can use the letter to spell the word on his strip, he can keep it. If not, he discards the letter. Keep passing the container around the group, allowing each child to pull one letter at a time, and see who can build his word first.

Compound Teamwork
VO–60 🖐

Create a list of compound words. Using index cards in two different colors, write one part of each compound word on one colored card and the other part of the compound word on the second color. Separate the decks by color. Group students into two teams and give each member of one team a card from one deck and the members of the other team cards from the second deck. At your signal, students from one team must pair themselves up with someone on the other team to make a compound word that is on your list.

For younger students, simplify this by writing each compound word on a geometric shape and then cutting it in half between the two words that make up the compound. Children match shapes to discover their compound word.

Once students have created real compound words, you might let them create nonsense compound words. For example, a child with a card that says *horse* teams up with a child who has *shoe* to make the word *horseshoe* in the first round. In the nonsense round, the child with *horse* might team up with a child whose card says *bow* (from *rainbow*). Together, they create the nonsense word *horsebow* and then write a definition and illustrate the new word.

⚓ Pop-up Flash Cards
VO-61 👁 🖐

Using the same format used to make pop-up books, make flash cards for kinesthetic learners by presenting them as pop-ups. Write the word to learn on the outside and have a pop-up picture on the inside for reinforcement.

Directions for pop-ups:

1. Fold a 5 x 8-inch index card in half.

2. Cut two 1-inch parallel slits on the folded edge.

3. Fold the cuts toward the open edge.

4. Crease.

5. Push the creased box into the inside opening.

6. Open to pop up.

7. Write the word to be learned on the outside and glue a picture inside.

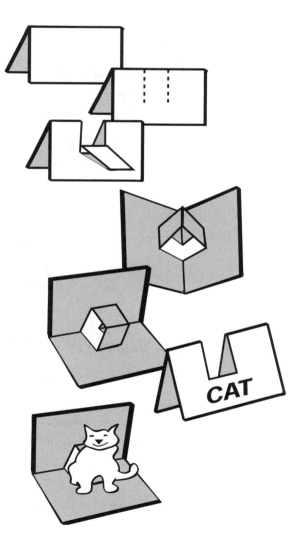

These can also be used to make vocabulary and definition pop-ups, sound and letter identification pop-ups, and even comprehension question pop-ups for character, plot, and setting.

What's My Word?
VO-62 ◆

This is similar to Words on a Walk (see p. 68) but instead of headbands, just attach a vocabulary word for review to each student's back. Use peel-off name tags or other sticky labels for this activity. In small groups or as a class, students walk around the room and ask each other questions to try to figure out what word they are wearing. You might instruct them to ask only questions that can be answered by *yes* or *no*, and you might also want to have a list of the words being used on the board. For example, for a unit on habitats, words might include *carnivore, prey, biome, shelter,* and *adaptations.* A student may ask: Am I a living thing? Am I a type of animal? Can living things stay alive without me?

Team Spirit
VO-63 ◉ ◆ ◆

List vocabulary words on the board and have two students stand or sit with their backs to the list. Read a definition for one of your listed words and at the count of three, students turn around and try to be the first to locate and call out the word that matches your definition. The winner earns a point for his team.

Make this activity more challenging by saying the word instead of the definition. The first student to locate the word must also give its meaning. If he is incorrect, the second student has a chance to define the word and earn a point for his team.

⚓ Word or Phrase Scrabble
VO-64 ◆

Use letter tiles or squares for this activity. Place enough letters to form all the words on your review list in a resealable plastic bag. Have students work in pairs. Each one pulls five letters from the bag and takes a turn trying to make a word from the list. If a student can't form a word using the first five letters, he may discard one of the letters (putting it back into the bag) and pull another letter from the bag. If he still can't make a word, his partner gets a turn. The students take turns until all the words have been formed.

Crossing the Creek
VO-65 🔁

Use this game with pairs or triads. Place new vocabulary or sight words on separate pieces of construction paper. The student spreads these papers out on the floor face up. The goal is for her to say each word and use it in a sentence as she steps on it while attempting to "cross the creek."

⚓ Artful Adjectives
VO-66 👁

Create a list of adjectives that lend themselves to artistic interpretation. Then give students paper, colored markers, and glitter markers, and ask them to draw the word to represent what it means. The word *spooky* will look mysterious, while the word *cold* should look as though it's shivering, and the word *glamorous* should look fancy and glittery. More adjectives to consider for this strategy include messy, bouncy, jittery, tiny, enormous, colorful, wide, and tall.

Cookies on My Mind
VO-67 👁 🔁

Create a set of laminated oak-tag gingerbread cookies for this activity. Write a vocabulary word on each cookie with a vis-à-vis marker and place the cookies in a cookie jar. Appoint one child to be "it." This child chooses a cookie and gives a definition for the word on the cookie. For example, if he chooses a cookie with the word *assist* on it, he might say, "I have a word that means 'to help.'" He chooses another child to guess the word that is written on the cookie. If the second child guesses the word, the student who is "it" asks him to spell or write the word. If the word is spelled or written correctly, the student earns the cookie. Now it is his turn to choose a cookie from the jar.

You can adapt this strategy for students who struggle with spelling by having them respond with only the first or last letters of the word. For math, you might write a number, a math problem, or even a simple word problem on a cookie.

⚓ Venn Vocabulary
VO-68 👁 ⚡

Have students use two intersecting Venn circles to compare and contrast new words. Younger students can focus on the structure of the two words, such as the number of syllables in each, the number of vowels, letters that the words have in common, whether they are compound words or words with a prefix or suffix, and so on. Older students will focus on the meanings of the words as well.

Nerf Words
VO-69 ⚡

Have one student toss a Nerf ball to a friend. The first student calls out a vocabulary word, and the student who catches the ball must define the word. If the second student answers correctly, she tosses the ball to a third student and calls out another word.

Allow struggling learners to keep word banks at their desks and refer to them.

Domino Vocabulary
VO-70 👁

Review words in a domino game by writing a word on half of an index card and placing a picture, not the matching picture, on the other half. Students lay out the cards and build off one another in domino fashion.

Comprehension

⚓ Magnetic Business Cards
CO-1 👁 🔦

Purchase magnetic business cards from an office supply store or make your own cards on the computer and simply attach a magnet. Show your students examples of real business cards and have a class or group discussion about the purposes and features of such cards.

Next, have each student take one or two cards and let her design a business card for a character in a book she is reading. What might the character choose for an illustration or graphic on his or her business card, based on what the author has told the reader? What kind of font would the character choose and what color ink would the card be printed in? What would the character include for a slogan? Students should be able to support the choices they make and the answers to these questions with examples from the text. Have students make a draft of their business cards on a small index card before they use the magnetic business card for their final draft. Have fine-point markers available for students to use.

Another way to use magnetic business cards is for sequencing events either in a story or in the content area. Sequencing is difficult for struggling readers. If they get one event out of sequence, the whole string of events needs to be rewritten. This strategy allows them to concentrate on the most important aspect of this task—determining sequence—without worrying about having to erase or start over. Write each event from a story on a separate card and place the cards on a magnetic surface. The student moves the cards around to arrange them in the correct sequence.

To use these in a content area, the process is the same. For example, write the steps in the water cycle or the events leading up to the American Revolution on the cards and have students arrange them in the correct order. Make this strategy self-checking so students can work on it as an anchor activity.

❧ Before and After
CO-2 👁

Before your students read a section of nonfiction text or a chapter or story from fiction, give them a list of statements related to the topic or story. Use the reproducible on page 180 for this organizer.

Ask them to check *I agree* or *I disagree* on the left side of each statement. Then have them read the text and reassess their opinions.

On the right side, they check *I agree* or *I disagree* again. At the bottom, ask them to write two facts they learned (from nonfiction) and to complete the statement *Two questions I still need answered*. Finally, have them complete the section *One thing I'm sure about.*.

Name _Marena Sabando_ **Topic or Title** _Volcanoes_

Read each statement below before you read the text and check I agree or I disagree in the columns on the left. After you have read the text, reread the statements and check I agree or I disagree in the columns on the right.

Before reading I agree	I disagree	Statements		After reading I agree	I disagree
✔		1.	There are volcanoes in Hawaii.		
✔		2.	Volcanic activity does not take place in extremely cold climates like the South Pole.		
	✔	3.	Volcanoes are good for farmers.		
	✔	4.	There is no active volcano in the U.S.		

Two facts I learned: 1. _____   2. _____

Two questions I still need answered: 1. _____   2. _____

One thing I'm sure about: _____

Prereading Strategies for Comprehension
CO-3

Always give children time to take a picture walk through a book to activate their prior knowledge, help them make personal connections to the story, and prime their brain for the reading to come.

As they look at illustrations, ask students some of the following questions:

- When do you think the story takes place? Could it be in the past, right now, or sometime in the future? What do you see that makes you think so?

- What season or time of the year could it be?

- Where do you think this story will take place?

- Who do you think some of the main characters will be?

- How do the pictures make you feel? How might the characters be feeling?

- Have you read any other stories by this author? Do the illustrations remind you of another book you have read?

- Is there a "blurb" or summary that tells you a little about this book? What does it say?

For younger readers, prereading strategies might also focus on one page of the text. To help orient young readers and get them ready to read, ask questions such as the following:

- Find the word *giant* on this page.

- Find a period on the page.

- Count the question marks you see on this page.

- What is the first word on the page? What is the last word?

- Find a word beginning with *p*.

- Find a word that means the same as *large*.

- Find a word that could be the name of a character in this book.

TIP

When you give struggling students comprehension questions to answer, include the page number where the answer can be located. For some students, you might need to take this a step further by placing a colored dot after the question and the same colored dot next to the paragraph where the answer can be found. Once the child has begun to experience success with this strategy, start pulling back to give her the page number only.

⚓ Two-Column Notes
CO-4 👁

Two-column notes are helpful for connecting students to the text. Use the organizer on page 181 in the reproducibles section. Model for students as you think aloud and list a few things you think you know about a new topic or story on the left-hand side of the organizer under *What I Might Know*. Then have students work alone or with a partner to do the same thing on their organizers. Next, have students read the assigned text. On the right-hand side, below *Facts I Can Show*, have students write the main ideas of the passage they have read or details that support or refute the statements they wrote in the left-hand column under *What I Might Know*.

Name _Joshua Bennett_   **Topic or Title** _Egyptian Pyramids_

What I Might Know:

Pyramids are made of sand.

Pyramids are as old as my Nana.

Pyramids hold treasures and mummies.

Facts I Can Show:

Pyramids are made from stone.

They are thousands of years old.

Kings and queens were sometimes buried

in them with things they would need in

the afterlife.

Partner Questions
CO-5

Pair students for partner reading and have partners stop after a paragraph, a page, or a chapter to ask each other a comprehension question or write a comprehension question for each other to answer. For nonfiction text, they should stop and ask questions after a section or subsection of text that focuses on a particular aspect of the content material.

⚓ Crossword Puzzles
CO-6 👁

Use this strategy instead of work sheets to assess comprehension and vocabulary knowledge. Write questions about a story or about content area information and record the answers in a crossword grid using centimeter graph paper or a software program for making crossword puzzles. Trace around the grid and distribute the blank numbered grids to the students along with the questions. There are also educational Web sites you can visit that have templates to use for crossword puzzles. To use as an anchor activity, provide the answers in a center so that students can self-correct their work.

READING MAINTENANCE FOR COMPREHENSION

Create this visual reference as a chart and display it where all students can see it and refer to it. You might also create the same information as a bookmark to give to students.

If I become confused—I need to read more to see if I understand.

If I want a preview of what's to come—I can speed ahead and skim for information.

If my brain is overloaded—I need to take a break, read more slowly, and make notes.

If I hit a wall on a word—I need to skip it, read on, and return to see what makes sense, look for context clues or picture clues, sound it out, look it up, or ask for help.

If I lose my train of thought and have no idea what I've read—I need to put on my brakes, retrace my steps, and figure out where the text stopped making sense.

If I need help—I should ask a friend or the teacher.

Who Am I?
CO-7 [C]

After reading a book or several chapters of a read-aloud, make cards with the names of characters and place them in a hat. A student chooses one and the others ask her *yes* or *no* questions to guess the name of the character that is written on her card. For example, if you are reading *The BFG* and a student chooses the card with *Sophie* on it, other students might ask her, "Are you a giant?" "Are you a girl?" "Do you live in an orphanage?"

King or Queen of the Hill
CO-8 [C]

Have a student sit on a designated "throne." Other students attempt to knock the king or queen off the throne with questions about content or comprehension. If the monarch can't answer a question, the student who asked it takes his place on the throne and is asked questions by other students.

⚓ Fishy Stories
CO-9

After reading a story, give students the outline of a fish body (see reproducible on p. 172) with vertical lines (bones) drawn on the inside of the fish. Children write the main events from the beginning to the end of the story on each of the bones to practice sequencing.

COMPREHENSION

Comprehension is the reason we read. Children who can decode but don't understand what they have read aren't really reading (making meaning out of words). Comprehension involves many skills, including prediction, inference, and understanding cause and effect. In addition to learning specific strategies for comprehension, students must also be taught to monitor their own comprehension. They must be aware of their thinking and be able to recognize when they don't understand what they are reading. Then they need to have "fix-it" strategies so they know how to resolve their comprehension difficulties.

Total Recall
CO-10

Teach your students the RCRC method of reading and retaining information. This makes a handy reference chart or bookmark for students, especially when they start reading nonfiction text.

> **R—Read.**
> Read a small part of the material. Read it again.
>
> **C—Cover.**
> Cover the written material with your hand or paper.
>
> **R—Retell.**
> Tell yourself what you read.
>
> **C—Check.**
> Lift the paper and check to see if you remembered it.

When you introduce this to children, make a bookmark for each student that has the same cues. Have reading partners practice the steps together by reading the same text, trying out each step, and coaching each other.

⚓ Handy Q and A
CO-11 👁 🖐

For activating prior knowledge before students read a passage, as well as for summarizing what they learned after reading, try this strategy. Give each child a blank sheet of paper. (If you have students with larger hands or students that just need more room to work, give them 12 x 18-inch paper.) Have them fold it like a book and then trace an outline of their left hands on the left side and their right hands on the right side of the fold. Next, they write their names on the left-hand palm and the topic they'll be reading about or the title of the story on the right-hand palm. On each finger of the left hand, they write a question about the topic or story. For example, if you are studying earth science, before they read about or have a lesson about volcanoes, have them list a question about volcanoes on each finger of the left hand. You can also have them record what they think they already know about the topic. On each finger of the right hand, they list a new fact they learned about volcanoes after the lesson or the reading.

Wisdom Walk
CO-12

To compare ideas, share insights, and resolve questions, invite your students to take a Wisdom Walk after the class has discussed a story or chapter from a book or learned about a topic. Give each student a sheet of paper and a clipboard. Remind them to have a pencil with them. Have them walk around the room while music is playing in the background. When you stop the music, they are to ask the student closest to them a question about the reading or content, or ask them to define a word or share what they learned or found most interesting. Give students a few minutes to jot notes about what they heard before you start playing the music again. When students have had time to share with at least three different classmates, call them back to their seats and ask them to tell you what they jotted down on their clipboards.

RAFT
CO-13

This strategy is a good one for differentiation. After reading either fiction or nonfiction, students choose (or you can assign) roles (R) for a project based on their reading. The students decide who the audience (A) will be for their project. It could be their parents, another class, the school board, etc. The format (F) is the final product they choose in order to demonstrate their understanding of the book or topic. They may decide to present a skit, write a song, do an art project, or anything else that will showcase their work and that you have given them permission to do. The topic (T) is the *who, what,* or *when* that is the focus of their project.

After reading about global warming, for example, the RAFT might look like this:

R = Take the role of a fortune-teller.

A = The audience will be listeners of National Public Radio.

F = The format will be a radio broadcast in which a fortune-teller is interviewed.

T = The final product will be a segment on an NPR program that will alert listeners to the dangers of global warming and ways they can curb global warming now.

SQ3R Study System
CO-14

This comprehension strategy and study technique focuses students on the purposes for reading nonfiction text.

• **S = Survey.**
Students read and survey headings in text. They examine any graphics, such as charts, diagrams, and photos, and read the introduction and summary. They notice bold-print words and think about what background knowledge related to this topic they already have.

• **Q = Question.**
Show students how to turn each heading and subheading into a question about the material they will be reading. For example, if they are going to read about the Civil War in a social studies text, and the heading for one section is "Reasons for War," they would ask themselves, "What were the reasons for the Civil War?"

• **3R = Read, Recite, Review.**
Teach students to read a section of text, and then recite it to themselves in their own words as they try to summarize the main points. Then they review what they read as they think about their thinking and whether they understood the material.

> **TIP**
>
> Collect "do not disturb" signs from hotels or make your own. Have students place them on their chairs or desks when they are involved in an assignment or project and don't want to be distracted.

When you introduce SQ3R, have students work in pairs to practice and coach each other through each step. Post the steps for reference and make bookmarks for students.

Question and Answer Relationships (QAR)
CO-15

Teach your students about the four different types of questions they are most likely to encounter in their daily work and in assessments of all kinds. Once they know where to look and how to find the answers to different kinds of comprehension questions, they are much more likely to answer the questions correctly. QAR teaches students to analyze the question that they are being asked.

• **Level 1 questions** are the literal questions that children can easily answer by looking at the text. They can usually point directly to answers for these "in the book" questions. They don't have to think about the question and how to answer it; they just need to find it in the text and copy it or repeat it.

• **Level 2 questions** are also in the book, but they aren't all together in the same sentence or even the same paragraph. They may even be spread over several pages or scattered throughout a chapter. They are sometimes referred to as "search and find questions" because students will need to scan the text they have read to locate the answer, which often has more than one component. For example, students who are reading about volcanoes might read a section about the Ring of Fire where most volcanic activity takes place. A Level 2 question might ask them to give the names of three countries that border the Ring of Fire and experience active volcanoes. Students would need to scan the text and perhaps look at maps or charts to answer this question. They would need to search to find the answer or answers.

• **Level 3 questions** are more difficult to answer because students need to read between the lines and add what they already know to what the author has written. In other words, these questions are often inferential. They are also referred to as "author and me" questions. Students have to draw on their background knowledge and combine that with what the author has told them to answer level 3 questions. An example would be fiction text about a child who moves to a new state and must make friends in her new school. Readers might be asked how the child is feeling, and they would draw on their understanding of how they have felt in a situation where they did not know anyone and combine that with what the author has told them to come up with an answer.

• **Level 4 questions**, often asked before students read a text, can be answered without reading the book at all. These are sometimes called "in my head" questions. All the student has to do is think about the question that she's being asked. There is no right or wrong answer and no reading is required to answer level 4 questions, so students like them. These questions are great for activating prior knowledge. If your students are going to read about hurricanes and tornados in a unit on weather, for example, you might ask them first if they have ever experienced a strong storm and how they felt when they knew a storm was on the way, what they did to prepare for it, and whether they saw any damage from the storm after it had passed. Discussing the topic beforehand gets students ready to read. It helps to activate their prior knowledge and helps them to make personal connections to the text.

❧ Character Bags
CO-16 👁

Give each student a white or brown lunch bag and have him decorate it with one character, setting, or event from a story that's being read. Pass the bags around to everyone in the class and ask each student to write a comment about the character, setting, or event, and place it in the bag. Bags go back to their designers, who read all the notes in their bags.

Students can also make a *define it* bag. They write a vocabulary word on the front of the bag, making it colorful and interesting with markers, and then pass it around in a small group until everyone has written a definition, description, synonym, or sentence using the word on a slip of paper and has placed it in the bag. For younger students, give them a word to write and have others write rhyming words or draw pictures of items that rhyme. This also works with initial sounds, blends, and other phonemes.

MORE COMPREHENSION STRATEGIES

When your students have completed a book or other reading, give them choices about how they will respond to what they have read. Here are a few popular ways that readers can respond to text that don't involve the usual book-report format.

• Design a "You Tube" clip that details the story.

• Design a "My Space" page for a main character or a historical figure.

• Compose a text message stating the main events or the beginning, the middle, and the end of the story. Allow students to write in text format without grading spelling. However, they must limit the size of their message.

• Use a phonics phone to call the main character and discuss the ending or plot. (This one is good for younger readers.) Students write a response to their calls in their journals or discuss it in the guided reading group.

• Compose a letter to the main character supporting an action that he or she took.

Always set the purpose for reading before students begin. Let them know what the focus and purpose of their reading should be. Ask multiple-choice comprehension questions occasionally. You may need to provide one correct answer for every two obviously incorrect answers until the student becomes comfortable with the process. Offer hints for less obvious questions if needed.

Comprehension Bingo
CO-17

Distribute papers with eight empty blocks on each one and ask children to write the titles of eight of their favorite books or stories, one per block, including books you've read to them. Let children work in small groups or with a buddy if they wish. This helps children who have trouble remembering titles or who struggle with encoding. Just remind them to write the titles in different boxes from where their partner writes them. Then give each child eight index cards. On each one, she writes a sentence about a character from each title she has listed. When students have finished, collect their cards and let the game begin. The caller reads a sentence card about a character and children who have listed the book title for that character cover the block with that title written in it with a bingo chip. The first student to cover all eight blocks is the winner and becomes the next caller.

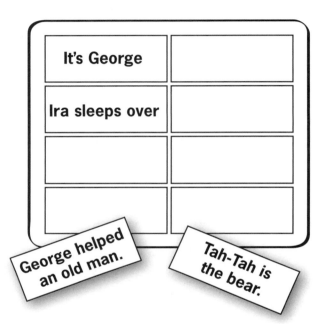

This works well with vocabulary words and definitions, too, and is a great way to review words before a quiz.

⚓ Building a Story Frame
CO-18

Some students need a frame of reference for writing a book report. Provide this before they read to facilitate their writing. Here's an example.

The title of the book was _____.

The problem was _____.

How everything worked out was _____.

If I could call someone from this story, it would be _____ and here's what I would say: _____.

If I could speak to the author, here's what I would say: _____.

⚓ QAD
CO-19 👁

Divide a paper into thirds. On the left-hand side (Q), the student writes questions he has about the assigned reading, or questions he wants to have answered. In the middle section (A), he writes answers he has found to those questions during or after the reading. On the right-hand side (D), he writes supporting details after reading.

⚓ Sentence Strip Sequence
CO-20 📧

Write a different event from a story on each of three sentence strips. Children manipulate the sentences to place them in the correct sequence. Number the strips on the back to make them self-correcting.

To make this a writing assignment, give students blank sentence strips and have them write the events and number the strips. Later, have students exchange sentence strips for sequencing.

TELLS: Fact or Fiction
CO-21 👁

Give students an acronym for reading comprehension that they can apply to fiction and nonfiction text.

> **T** = **Title.** Look at the title for clues about the story or the passage.
>
> **E** = **Examine.** Examine the text for visuals—illustrations, diagrams, charts—or word clues to help you understand what you are going to read.
>
> **L** = **Look.** Focus in on key words, heads or subheads, or visuals and write down any that you think are important. In nonfiction, these words are often in bold print and in a glossary, if one is included.
>
> **L** = **Look again.** If you wrote down key words, look them up or ask for help if you don't know their meanings. Check for context clues.
>
> **S** = **Setting.** Always identify the where and the when in your reading.

Line Cueing
CO-22 👁

When you are testing students on content or vocabulary, give struggling students this cue. Provide a separate, short line for each letter in the answer to a question. For example, if the answer to a question on your science quiz is *volcano*, draw seven short lines, one for each letter in the word, in the space where the student will write his response.

⚓ Prediction Maps
CO-23 👁

Have students create a map that begins with a prediction they write about a character or plot in the book they are reading. Next, they list the information they know from their reading that caused them to make the prediction. Then they continue to read to figure out whether or not their prediction was accurate.

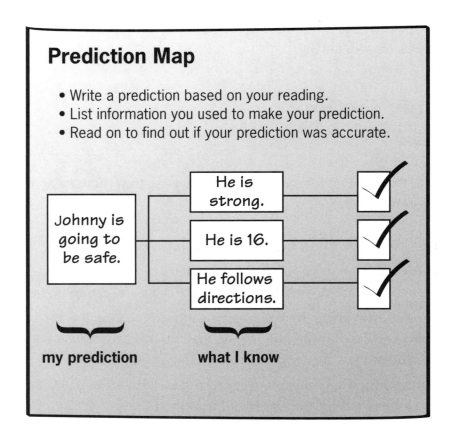

Prediction Map

- Write a prediction based on your reading.
- List information you used to make your prediction.
- Read on to find out if your prediction was accurate.

Johnny is going to be safe.	He is strong.	✓
	He is 16.	✓
	He follows directions.	✓

my prediction — what I know

⚓ KWL, KWL+
CO-24

This popular strategy models the metacognitive thinking necessary for effective reading, while actively involving students with print. Give students, partners, or groups paper that is held landscape style and divided into three columns. They write K at the top of the left hand column for What I Know, W at the top of the middle column for What I Want to Know, and L at the top of the column on the right, for What I Learned.

Introduce the topic and ask students to write everything they know about it under K and everything they want to know about it under W. Then teach the lesson or assign the reading students will do. After they complete the reading or lesson, they write everything they've learned under the L section. This strategy is effective for content area reading as well as literature.

For variety, add the plus sign for KWL+. In this version, the paper is divided into four columns and the last column on the right-hand side is labeled with a plus sign. The columns for K, W, and L are filled out the same as above, but in this version, the last column on the right that is labeled with a plus sign is for students to write anything they would still like to know about the topic.

> **TIP**
>
> For a fast comprehension check, try an activity called Zip Around or Pass. Go around a group or the whole class and ask each student to add a comment or observation about a character in a book, an event, or the plot. A student may say "pass," but you will return to him after everyone in the group has added a comment and expect him to contribute.

⚓ Pocket Phrases
CO-25 🔖 👁

Glue six library card pockets on a folder. Write *who, what, where, when, why,* and *how* on the pockets. Cut apart sentences that you've copied from a story and ask students to match the phrases with the correct pockets, placing the strips inside each one. For example, if your students are reading "The Story of the Three Little Pigs," the phrase *once upon a time* would go in the *when* pocket, *three little pigs* would go in the *who* pocket, along with *big bad wolf*, and *house of straw* would go in the *what* pocket with *house of sticks* and *house of bricks*.

Listening Comprehension Bingo
CO-26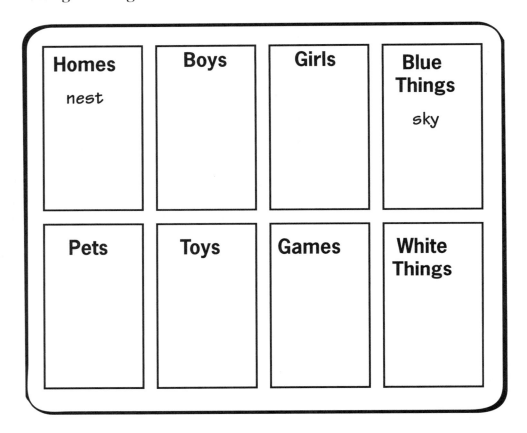

Before you read a book to a guided reading group or to the class, prepare a grid with eight sections or blocks for each child. In each block, write the name of a category from the story or text you will read. If you're reading about birds, for example, one category might be *homes*. When you read the word *nest* in the story, students write that word in the box labeled *homes*. The first individual or group to complete their grid is congratulated and awarded the title of best listener of the day.

Homes	Boys	Girls	Blue Things
nest			sky
Pets	Toys	Games	White Things

Wheel of Fortune
CO-27

Ask students to write down key words or ideas from assigned reading. Use these ideas to make a Wheel of Fortune game. After the class participates in the fun, keep the student-generated ideas for the test you might give later. For example, after reading *Naomi Knows It's Springtime* by Virginia Kroll, one child might write *another word for ice cream*. Another child guesses alphabet letters to fill in the word *custard*.

Cube It!
CO-28 ▨

Use foam cubes, buy white-board cubes from a craft store, or make your own using the pattern on page 171. Cover each side with sunshine faces numbered from 1 to 6. On a separate sheet of paper, number from 1 to 6 and on each numbered line, list a different way students can report on what they've read. A student tosses the cube and refers to the paper to find the way he will report. See More Comprehension Strategies on page 97 and Children's Choice on page 105 for ideas for your list.

To use this activity with vocabulary words, on the separate sheet you might write:

1. Give a synonym for the word.

2. Give an antonym for the word.

3. Give two examples of the word.

4. Use the word in a sentence.

5. Tell how many syllables the word has.

6. Give a definition for the word.

Students in small groups or with a partner get a list of vocabulary words and toss the cube to find out how to respond to each word on the list. They give the answer orally in the group or with a partner.

Text Highlighting
CO-29 ◉

TIP

Help students set goals and get motivated to read with this strategy. Give each one an empty recipe file box and a stack of index cards. Ask them to "guesstimate" how many books they can read by a given date and write each student's guess on the top or front of his file box. Every time the student reads a book, he fills out a card with the title, author, characters, and setting, plus his favorite part, and places it in the file box. This practice inspires students to work toward reaching and beating their goals in the designated time frame.

Many struggling readers experience success when text material is highlighted in a consistent pattern for them. You might use blue highlighting tape for definitions, yellow for specific facts, and pink for main ideas. (Highlighting tape is available through Crystal Springs Books.) Decide on your color-coding key and post a reference chart in the classroom. Share the task of highlighting with colleagues. One teacher might highlight science texts for both classes while another highlights social studies books. Many teachers find that they only have to highlight one or two books a year. The tape is easily removed and saved on a laminated folder for future use.

Mapping a Story
CO-30 👁

Use a story map or graphic organizer to improve comprehension. Place a blank map on an overhead, chart, or PowerPoint page and ask students to complete the basic questions. Then apply their responses to more difficult comprehension questions. Map outlines might include who, where, when, identify the main problem, the goal, the actions needed to reach the goal, and the final outcome. For some students, you may need to model using the map in a mini lesson and work toward the goal of students completing maps independently. Other students might need to complete a map by using questions that are taped, by tape-recording their responses, or by having a study buddy fill in the blanks for them.

This strategy for understanding can also be used during the reading process, with the teacher allowing students to fill in their maps as they go along. See pages 182 to 188 for examples of story maps and other graphic organizers. Mapping is also a great way for students to think about and plan their writing.

⚓ Puzzling Envelopes
CO-31 👁 🔧

Give each student a 6 x 9-inch manila envelope with a clasp or string closure. The student first decorates the front of the envelope with a scene from a story or a chapter from a book she has read. She also writes the title and author clearly on the front of the envelope. Next, she takes a 9 x 12-inch piece of oak tag and illustrates a favorite scene from the story. The teacher laminates the picture, if desired, and the student carefully cuts it apart to make a puzzle. The puzzle pieces are placed inside the envelope and the finished envelopes are passed around the class for peers to assemble. Later, place these in a basket in your library area so children can use them again or go through them when they are looking for a title they might like to read.

A variation is to have the students write vocabulary words, such as new words related to a content area, along with their definitions on the oak tag. Then follow the directions above to create puzzles. For a writing activity, students write a letter to a friend on the oak tag, cut to make a puzzle, and drop the pieces in the envelope.

❦ Pick the Nose
CO-32

Draw a big nose on oak tag and laminate it. After reading an article, direct your students to summarize it on a single 3-inch square sticky note. Next, have the students write questions about the article on another sticky note. They save their summaries in a folder or book and place their sticky note questions on the large, laminated nose. As an anchor activity or when you have a few minutes between transitions, a student "picks the nose" and removes a sticky note. She reads the question and tries to answer it. If she's doing this as an anchor activity, she writes her answer on another sticky note and places it alongside the question on the nose. If you're doing the activity as a class, she gives the answer orally. If she needs help, the student who created the question pulls out his summary sticky note and helps her.

CHILDREN'S CHOICE

Having choices is highly motivating to students. Instead of writing book reports, let a student choose one of the following, but encourage a different choice each time a new book is read.

- Draw a mural depicting the main idea.

- Create sentence strips with illustrations that represent the sequence of events.

- Create a newspaper article about the book with a headline supporting the main idea. Add a captioned illustration.

- Write a friendly letter to a character telling that character what he did in the book that you approved of or disapproved of.

- Illustrate a movie poster that advertises the book. Tell who each character will be played by.

- Dress up in costume as the main character and tell the story in your own words.

- Videotape a TV commercial advertising why other students should read it.

- Make a greeting card for the author.

- Develop a comic strip that depicts the main events or a different ending.

- Create a different book jacket.

- Write to the author and tell her why she should write a sequel to the book and why you should be the main character in the next book.

⚓ Little Hula Hoop Venns
CO-33 ⬉

Use small table-top hula hoops or embroidery hoops and small sticky notes for this comprehension strategy. Give students two vocabulary words, concepts, characters, or stories to compare and contrast. They work independently to make notes on small stickies and then use them with the hula hoops to create a Venn diagram.

Sticky-Note Summary
CO-34

When a student has trouble processing long passages of text, try chunking it into smaller amounts. Give him a sticky note after he has read a page or a short section of text and have him summarize the story, or give you the gist of a passage, using the front of the sticky note only. Then after he has read another chunk, give him a second sticky note. Save all the notes he writes for the story or chapter in a folder for review when he has completed the reading.

⚓ Comprehension Tic-Tac-Toe
CO-35 👁

Use the Tic-Tac-Toe reproducible on page 190 to give students choices in how they react to stories or books that they read. They will need to do three activities in a row just like Tic-Tac-Toe.

Question Tags
CO-36

A strategy that is especially helpful for students with comprehension weaknesses is to tag their text with comprehension questions you have written on sticky notes before they read. Place a question tag on each page or every other page, depending on the text. Have the student write his response on the note and leave it on the page so you can check in with him.

⚓ Big Hula Hoop Venn Characters
CO-37 🔧

Have partners or small groups of students work together on the rug with two large hula hoops and 3-inch sticky notes for this strategy. They create a Venn diagram with the hoops and write on the sticky notes as they compare and contrast two characters from a story, such as Frog and Toad from the books by Arnold Lobel or for older students, Pink and Say from the book with the same title by Patricia Polacco.

⚓ AHA! Connections
CO-38 👁

When students make connections to text they are reading, good things happen for their comprehension. Use the reproducible on page 191 or give students a paper to fold in half vertically. Have them label the left-hand column *My AHA Moments* and the right one *My Connections.* As they read, they jot down in the left-hand column notes about words, characters, events, or ideas that spark a response for them or catch their eye. In the right-hand column, they jot notes about the connections to their own lives that made the "AHA!" moment happen.

> **TIP**
>
> Address a pack of 4 x 6-inch blank index cards to school friends such as the principal, nurse, guidance counselor, and other teachers. Each month the children read a book of their choice, pick an addressed "postcard," and draw a character, scene, or a new book cover on the front of the card. They write a brief book summary on the back and deliver their mail to the person named on the front of the card.

Show Me State(ment)
CO-39 📷

Instead of giving your students assignments in workbooks, written tests, or work sheets, encourage them to take a proactive role in their learning with this strategy. One child stands in front of a group and says, "Tell me two ways chapter 7 might end" or "Tell me two sentences that express surprise." Other group members offer answers and ideas, and then another student gets a turn. With younger learners, you might encourage students to say, "Find two objects that begin with the letter *g*" or "Give me two words that rhyme with *dog.*" Students must base their questions or statements on the reading they are doing or on a topic that they are studying in social studies, science, or math.

Listen Up
CO-40 🕮

When you read a story to a group or to the class, have a large poster in view that shows a web to help students listen for specific information, such as the main character, other characters, the sequence of events, the setting, the problem, and the solution. See the reproducible on page 188 for a web to use as a model or with individual students.

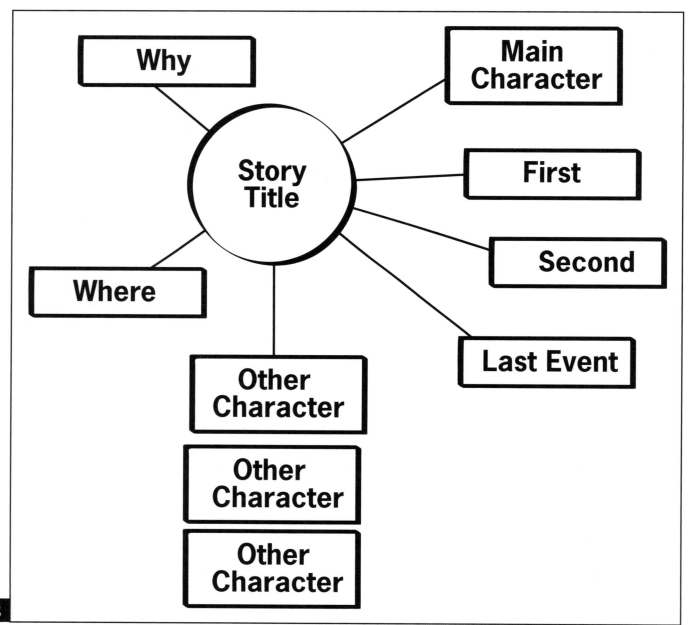

⚓ True and False Spiders
CO-41 👁 ✒

Draw a big spider body on a sheet of paper and write a statement about content area information or a character or an event from a story on the body. Have your students attach eight legs to the spider on which they have written sentences that either substantiate or refute the statement on the spider's body. If your class is studying weather, for example, you might write the following statement on the spider's body: Hurricanes are more dangerous than tornados. Students should use the information from their text or lesson to write their sentences. They must identify each statement they write as true or false.

Go Fish
CO-42 👁 ✒

Write questions on a school of cutout fish and keep them handy in a fishbowl on your desk. (See p. 172 for a reproducible to use.) The questions can be based on thematic units students have completed. You can also use comprehension questions from your read-aloud book or other reading, or vocabulary words from a content area. Use this activity to prime their brains for a unit to come as well. They'll be activating prior knowledge for future learning. When children need a filler activity, they can catch a fish and answer the question by applying reading-to-learn strategies.

> **TIP**
>
> Have you ever wondered what to do with leftover skills work sheets? Fill in the answers, then cut them apart so that the questions and answers are separated. Laminate them and attach a small magnet to the back of each piece. Use a cookie sheet for the backboard. Have the students manipulate the strips of paper to reassemble the work sheet and read the correct answers.

Prediction Wand
CO-43 📢 ✒

Have students sit in a circle as you read to them. Give them a glittery wand to pass around the circle. Stop reading without warning and ask the student who is holding the wand to predict what will happen next in the story. If you can find something that resembles a crystal ball, such as a glass sphere or ornamental lawn "gazing globe," the student holding it becomes the fortune-teller who predicts the future and what will happen in the story. Use this strategy in guided reading groups, too.

Story Clouds
CO-44 [C]

Use this activity to help students recall and retell a story you've read in guided reading groups or as a read-aloud. List for parents the activity's goals and the steps necessary for its completion. Choose a story to read to the class or group and photocopy in black and white an illustration from the book. Make copies of the illustration for students. After reading the story to the children, give each child a cloud cutout with the illustration on one side of it. The child takes the story cloud home and retells the story to his parents. They write the story on the cloud as the child dictates it and the child colors the illustration and returns the cloud to school. Display the finished clouds on sky-blue bulletin board paper.

Condensed Version
CO-45 [C]

Pair students and give them a paragraph from a newspaper or magazine at their instructional level. Together, they read the paragraph and condense it to five sentences that tell all the important facts, including *who, what, where, when,* and *how.* Give them index cards or large sticky notes to reinforce the concept of condensing, or shrinking, the information to give the gist of the article.

❧ Put the Fun in Functional
CO-46 👁

Even our younger readers are being asked to respond to comprehension questions based on functional literacy in formal assessments. Use this strategy to give them experience with this type of questioning. Save labels or boxes from products children enjoy. Some examples are candy wrappers, toy packaging, and boxes that granola bars or other treats come in. Design questions based on these packages that invite children to "read to learn." For example, ask them how many items a package contains, how many ounces a candy bar weighs, how many ingredients are listed on the ingredients panel, and other questions they can answer by looking carefully at the packaging.

Cause and Effect Tag
CO-47 [c]

Students will work with a partner for this comprehension strategy. Prepare sentences or phrases for each pair of students in your group. Each sentence or phrase should describe an event in a story they have read. The first student reads the sentence or phrase to the second student, who must finish it by saying *why* the event happened. For example, if the first student reads "Shelley got her umbrella," then the second student would say, "…because it was raining." If the sentence is "Dino got a bone," the second student would respond, "…because he learned to roll over." Students take turns reading the sentences and giving the reasons. If they get stuck or have a difference of opinion, they should go back to the story the sentences are based on.

When they have completed their set of sentences or phrases, they exchange them with another pair of students and do the next set. You may also want to have students write the new sentences they form and highlight the cause part and the effect part in different colors. Later, have students work together to write cause and effect sentences based on another class read-aloud or a book that all students will be familiar with.

TIP

Draw a hopscotch grid on the floor or block one out with masking tape. Label each block with a specific category, such as compound words, storybook characters, or animals that migrate. Have students toss a coin onto the grid. They look to see what category is written in the grid where their coin landed and then they try to list as many items in that category as possible in 20 seconds. They are competing against themselves to break their own records in this activity.

Jeopardy for Readers
CO-48 [s]

Use this strategy to help students learn about *wh* questions. Design a game board based on a particular story, with five columns of categories and five or more rows of answers. Cover the squares with "funny money" (see p. 169) or actual prizes the students can win, such as homework passes or new pencils. The child chooses a square, reveals the answer, and then must ask the question that goes with the answer. Here's an example.

Category: Pets

Answer: Buster

Question: What was Ryan's dog named?

⚓ Top It Off
CO-49 👁

Students use this folder activity to practice identifying the main topic of an article or story. Gather short stories or articles from students' readers, weekly news magazines that your class receives, or content area texts. Copy and glue the articles to the front of file folders. Students choose a folder, read the passage, and write the main idea plus the topic sentence and supporting details inside the folder. Provide an answer key on the back of the folder.

Scaffold this activity for struggling readers by creating multiple choice answers on the inside of the folder or providing sentence stems, such as:

- The main idea of this passage is…
- The sentence that tells me this says…
- A detail about the main idea is that…

Walk and Talk
CO-50 📇

Put a small amount of tempera paint in a dishpan. Have each student dip a bare foot into the paint, then put her foot on the center of a piece of construction paper. Laminate the dry footprints and place them on the floor around the room. Write *beginning*, *middle*, and *end* on them, and have the students walk and talk about the parts of different stories they have read. You can also write vocabulary words on each print and have students step on each word they can use in a sentence or define as they walk.

If you'd rather not deal with bare feet and paint, cut foot shapes from an Ellison die machine if there is one in your district.

Amnesia
CO-51 🎯

After studying a topic or reading a story, choose a child to "experience amnesia." He sits in the class rocking chair, facing away from his classmates. You hold up a vocabulary word from the unit of study you've just completed or the story you've read, making sure your amnesia victim can't see it. The child's classmates then give him clues to see if they can help the student guess the correct term and recover his memory. You could also use story plot and character clues for this activity.

Character Interviews
CO-52 🎯

After reading a story to your students, model what it might be like to be the main character and be interviewed by someone. Choose a student to interview you or another adult if one is available. Then divide students into pairs and have them set up interviews for their favorite characters. Brainstorm with the class questions they might ask based on a book they are all familiar with and post some of these questions on a chart to help students get started. One student is the interviewer and the other student role-plays the main character. Then they switch roles the next time. If possible, videotape the interviews and play them back in class, both for the students' enjoyment and for visitors. Have them available for viewing by parents waiting at conference time.

TIP

Purchase inexpensive paper gift bags with handles or ask parents to donate used bags. Decorate the front of each bag with a picture or scene from a favorite grade-level book. Inside each bag, place a paperback copy of the book and two or three activity cards hooked together on a ring. When a student chooses that book to read, ideas for activities are already included.

Toss Up
CO-53 📝

Label a blank die or cube with *who, what, where, when, why,* and *how.* Students work in pairs or small groups to answer the question that lands on top when they toss the die. This can be used with fiction and social studies texts and is great for reviewing current events articles that students read about in weekly magazines at their levels.

Character Corners
CO-54 ⬗

To encourage students to think about their thinking as they read, label each corner of the classroom with the name of a character from a book you're reading together. For example, for *Charlotte's Web*, you might label corners *Charlotte*, *Fern*, *Wilbur*, and *Mother*. In addition, create a poster with the following statements:

- "I agree because …"
- "I disagree because …"
- "I would have …"
- "The author could have …"

Display the poster in the front of the room. Prepare statements about the book to read to students and, on your signal, have students go to the corners that match their opinions. For example, you might ask students who they think is the strongest character in chapter 4. After a brief think time, they go to the corner of their choice. Once they've decided where to stand, ask one or two students in each corner to explain why they chose as they did. They may use the sentence starters on your poster if they wish. You can also ask students which character is most like them. They go to the corresponding corner and tell you why they think the character is like them.

This is also a good activity when you want to get students to predict what might happen next in a story. Give students four possible outcomes of a story, assign a corner for each one, and then after think time, students go to the corner they think is the real outcome of the story. They should always tell you how they decided and what in the text helped them to make their decisions. (Char Forsten calls this "voting with your feet.")

WRITING

Sentences and Paragraphs (SP)

Mechanics (ME)

Revising and Editing (RE)

General Strategies for Writing Success

- Collect interesting, colorful illustrations from magazines and clip art and keep them in a box or folder. When students have difficulty thinking of a topic for writing, invite them to look through the pictures.

- Use an empty aquarium and label it the Think Tank. On cutout fish, write story ideas or other writing topics. When students are stumped for writing ideas, invite them to visit the Think Tank. (Use the fish patterns on p. 172.)

- For students who are easily overwhelmed by writing assignments, try giving them the option of writing captions. Take photos of students, guests, school activities, and so on. Place them in a photo album. Give the student 3-inch square sticky notes and have him write captions for some of the illustrations.

- Be sure to offer students a wide variety of writing experiences. Recipes, directions for a favorite game, a review of their favorite movie or TV show, or a letter to a friend are all valid alternatives to writing a story.

- Variety is the spice of life. Let students write with pens and markers, and give them all kinds of options for paper. Collect decorated printer paper when it's on sale and ask parents or local businesses to donate stationery.

- Some students are more comfortable writing on the floor or with a slant board or lap desk. Give them options for where they can write.

- Occasionally let students collaborate for writing.

- Encourage shorter pieces and a variety of types of writing—poetry, riddles, letters to authors, characters, or pen pals. Try to limit bed-to-bed stories that go on for several pages. Less is more, and quality trumps quantity.

- When you notice students relying on worn-out words such as nice, good, and pretty, write the words on blank, white index cards cut to look like gravestones. Post them on a bulletin board and title it "RIP Words."

- Place a pencil inside the holes of a whiffle-type golf ball for young writers. The ball provides them with a more relaxed grip on the pencil.

- Provide opportunities for students to share their writing with peers and students from other grades. Have a writers' tea and invite parents. Let students showcase their best work.

Sentences and Paragraphs

❦ Flip and Mix
SP–1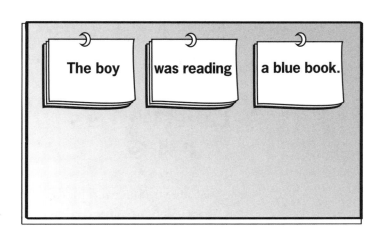

Use a piece of 8 x 20-inch oak tag for a backboard. Punch three holes in the top, about 6 inches apart. Use 3 x 5-inch index cards and write one part of a sentence on each one. (Add illustrations for emergent readers.) Punch holes in the top of the cards and hook them through the holes on the backboard. Children flip different cards to mix and match parts and make sentences. They choose one real sentence that makes sense to copy and illustrate and another nonsense sentence to copy and illustrate. Both sentences must tell a complete thought.

Graphing Word Usage
SP–2 👁

A student who uses the same words over and over in his writing can benefit from this strategy. Create a graph using 1-inch graph paper or use the form on page 189. Skim the student's writing and make a list of his most overused words. List the words along the horizontal axis at the bottom of the graph and the numbers 1 to 6 on the vertical axis. Give the student a highlighter and ask him to go through his piece of writing and highlight each instance of the first word listed on the graph, then count how many times he used it, and color in the graph to represent that number. Then he uses another color to highlight the next word. When he's done, show him how to use a thesaurus or word wall to find other words he can use instead of the words on his graph. (Also, see Wrap-It-Up Word Bank on p. 119.) Have the student add some of the new words to his writing folder or a personal word wall.

❧ Pocket Sentences
SP-3 ▨

Glue three library card pockets along the top of an open file folder. Code each pocket with a colored dot. Then create phrase strips and color-code them to match. Students choose a strip from each pocket and assemble a sentence. Have them write their new sentences on separate sheets of paper. Then they put the strips back into the matching pockets and choose again to make a different sentence.

❧ Label Writers
SP-4 ◉

When you have a reluctant writer, try this strategy. Give her a colorful poster or picture from a magazine that has a lot of detail and a stack of mini size sticky notes. Have her label as many parts of the picture or poster as she can. When you have checked her work and asked her about her labels, move the stickies onto a blank sheet of paper and have the student write a story using as many of the words on the stickies as she can. Instead of having her rewrite the words, let her place the stickies in her story rebus-style.

❧ Vocab-Acrostic
SP-5 ◉

Students who find writing difficult have success with acrostic poems. Students write vocabulary words vertically on a sheet of notebook paper. Using the letter on each line, they write a phrase or a sentence that explains or describes the vocabulary word. They may use a synonym, an example, a descriptive word or phrase, a definition, or a sentence.

A simple acrostic poem for the word *prey* might look like this:

Predator eats this.

Rabbits are prey for coyotes.

Even large animals like deer can be prey.

Yellowstone National Park has predators called wolves.

Round Robin Stories
SP-6

To give students practice writing clear and effective paragraphs, try this strategy. Have students work in groups of five to seven. Give each student a 5 x 8-inch index card. Each student writes a topic sentence for a paragraph on her card. At your signal, all students pass their cards to the student on their left. Each student reads the topic sentence on the card she gets and writes one sentence that supports the topic sentence on the card she has received. At your signal, students again pass their cards to the student on their left and repeat the process. When each card reaches the student who wrote the original topic sentence, that student reads the paragraph on her card and writes a concluding sentence. Give students a chance to share their paragraphs with other groups or as a whole class. Talk about what made paragraphs interesting. Copy a few of them on a blank transparency and share them with the class.

Wrap-It-Up Word Bank
SP-7

To encourage students to use the most descriptive words possible in their writing, wrap two boxes in wrapping paper. Cover one box with wrinkled, plain brown paper and the other with beautiful gift wrap. Place ordinary adjectives like *good*, *nice*, and *pretty* in the brown box. In the fancy box, keep more specific, descriptive adjectives like *kindhearted*, *exuberant*, and *vivacious*. Invite children to choose adjectives from this box to make their writing more interesting. Caution students to check a word they choose in a dictionary or a thesaurus to make sure the word means what they want to say in their writing.

To help children become aware of interesting words when they are reading independently, give them strips of paper and ask them to record any interesting words they come across to add to the elegantly wrapped box. Have them share the words and talk about their meanings with the class before adding them to the box—a great way to begin a writing session! You may want them to note on the strip of paper the book title and page number where they found the word so you can refer to it later if the child doesn't understand the word's meaning.

⚓ Character Acrostics
SP-8 👁

Have the students choose their favorite character from a read-aloud book, from their independent reading, or from a guided reading selection. Instruct them to write the character's name, letter by letter, vertically down the side of a piece of lined paper. Then show them how to create a character acrostic by modeling this with the name of your favorite character. Next, have them write phrases about the character, using the letters of the character's name as the beginning letter in each line of the acrostic. Each line must be a detail about the character that can be supported with information from the text.

Kite Tales
SP-9 🔦

When students need to work on writing paragraphs, try this strategy. Let students make kite shapes out of construction paper. Then, using their suggestions and ideas, write a topic sentence for a paragraph on the body of each kite. Have each student choose a kite shape with a topic sentence written on it. Give the students strips of paper to use for kite tails, and have them write three to five supporting details for their topic sentence, one on each strip of paper. Have them attach the supporting detail "tails" to the body of the kite with a piece of yarn and tape.

⚓ Writing Dialogue
SP-10 👁

When students need to practice writing dialogue, try this appealing strategy. Cut pictures of people or animals from magazines and glue them onto sheets of paper to look like they're facing each other. Draw "speech bubbles" as you would for a comic strip above the characters' heads. (Make extra copies of these to have at a writing center, too. Children love them.) Invite students to create what the characters are saying to each other and record their words in the speech bubbles. Use these for teaching punctuation in dialogue, too. Let children work in pairs to read their dialogues aloud to the class. Remind them to practice so they'll sound fluent.

Who's in the Beginning, Middle, and End?
SP-11

Write 10 to 15 detailed sentences on a piece of paper. Divide each sentence into a beginning, middle, and end. Write each part of each sentence on a separate 5 x 8-inch index card. Mix up the cards and distribute them to the class. On your signal, the students mingle to find the classmates with the two missing pieces of their sentence. Once they find their sentence-mates, they line up so that the parts of their sentence are in the right order.

Most Wanted
SP-12

Students love to create a "wanted poster" for a character from a story. After they've drawn the character's picture or mug shot, they'll need to write a careful description of the character, including what he looks like as well as how he behaves. They'll also need to support what they write with proof from the story in which the character appeared.

Exciting Slices
SP-13

TIP

To remind students to check their work before they hand it in, make a COPS poster and display it where students will place their completed work. The C is for capitalization, the O is for organization (have they set up their paper according to your directions with their name, date, and class?), the P is for punctuation, and the S can stand for spelling or sentence structure, depending on your focus.

Collect clean, empty pizza boxes from a local pizzeria. You'll need one for each student. Each child draws a picture of herself and attaches it to the cover of the box. On a pizza-sized circle of oak tag or construction paper, she then writes and illustrates six to eight sentences or paragraphs that represent "slices" of her life. These could include milestones such as moving to a new city, getting a pet, the arrival of a sibling, and so on.

Use the same concept for a book review. On the outside of their boxes, the students draw pictures of the most memorable scenes. On the inside "pizza," they write and illustrate summaries of each scene to create a synopsis. To use the strategy with nonfiction text, have students draw and summarize the steps in a process or events in the life of a historical figure.

⚓ Proud-to-Be-Me Book
SP–14 👁

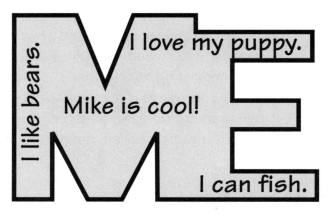

Cut the shape of the word *ME* out of heavy oak tag or poster board. Give students their own *ME* shape and invite them to decorate it and write descriptive phrases about themselves to help peers learn more about each other. Bind all of your students' *ME* books together for a handy classroom directory.

⚓ Gallery Walk
SP–15 🖎 👁

Use this strategy as a review technique or to share knowledge. Hang five to seven large sheets of chart paper in the classroom or hallway. Label each one with a topic. Give the students markers and encourage them to write their comments about each topic. Have them initial their responses or write their first names. That way, you can also use it as an informal assessment or as a preassessment, if you do it before you begin a unit of study. For example, you might tell students that in a few weeks, you'll begin a unit on rocks and minerals. They write what they already know or think they know about this topic. Don't worry if some of their comments are not accurate. They are still activating background knowledge and writing. There will be opportunities later for revising inaccuracies.

Another way to use this strategy is to label the charts according to the skills you want children to practice. If you want them to practice vocabulary, you might label one chart *compound words*, another chart *words with prefixes*, a third *words with suffixes*, and so on. For younger students, label each chart with an initial or ending sound or CVC words. For example, if you labeled a chart "Draw something that has 3 phonemes," children would draw a cat, dog, boat, and so on.

⚓ Tri-fold Stories
SP-16 👁

After they have completed a book, help students wrap up the story. Cut oak tag into 6 x 24-inch strips. Fold each strip into thirds that are 8 inches wide to create a little book. The three sections represent the beginning, middle, and end of the story. Attach a colorful ribbon to the outside of the book so that when the strip is folded, the ribbon can be tied to keep the book closed. Distribute the books. Have students write the title of the book and the author and illustrator on the front of the book, as well as their own names. The students untie the ribbons, open up the books, and design the three parts for the story as they wish.

After they've finished their books, they can tie them together again and share them with other students in the class. Place these in the classroom library for students to reread and have them available for parents to enjoy while they are waiting for conferences at back-to-school nights.

⚓ Before and After Story
SP-17 👁

Ask each student to bring a favorite photo to school. Bring in some of your own photos as well. Display the photos in a learning center. Have students select a photo other than their own and write sentences telling what they think might have happened *before* and *after* the picture was taken. If appropriate, teach them to use cue words for sequencing in their writing, such as *first, next, then, after,* and *finally.* Share the stories with the class and let the students who brought in the photos tell the real *before* and *after* of their photos.

⚓ Writing Letters
SP-18

Choose four or five alphabet letters each week and post them on the bulletin board. When you have a few minutes, ask the children to write sentences using all four letters. For example, *A, B, C,* and *D* might become the sentence *Always Buy Cream Doughnuts.*

⚓ Paragraph Frames
SP-19

Students who have difficulty starting to write may benefit from having a frame or format in their writing folders. The sentence stems give them confidence and supply needed cues about organization. See the example below.

Dogs make great pets. First of all, dogs are_____. Another reason I like dogs is that _____. Unlike cats, dogs _____. I would rather have a dog than any other kind of pet because _____.

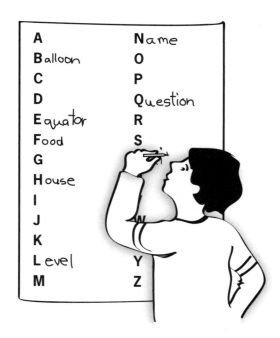

Use a student's informal interest inventory to create frames based on his favorite sports, hobbies, and interests. (See p. 167 for an informal interest inventory you can use.) Some students may also need a word bank when they are given a specific topic to write about.

⚓ A to Z Review
SP-20 👁

Upon completing a thematic unit or reading selection, hand each student a piece of paper with the alphabet written vertically along the side in two columns. (See illustration.) Students work independently, with a partner, or in groups to see how many words from the unit or book they can recall that begin with each letter.

⚓ Main Idea Puzzles
SP-21 ◤

Reinforce the concept of main ideas in writing and reading with this activity. On a piece of card stock, write a main idea or topic title. Underneath the main idea, write a topic sentence, three to five supporting detail sentences, and a concluding sentence, if applicable. Cut apart the sentences, place them in an envelope or plastic bag, and have students reassemble the pieces to make a

rting sentences in the

reverse side so that

liers, or sentences that don't

entify these outliers and

TIP

How many of us enjoy reading the message boards at the national conferences we attend? Children enjoy reading message boards, too. Designate a large bulletin board in a hall or in your wing of the school where children may write and read messages from peers and reading buddies in other classes.

practice

marks.

p. Cut out

ve the

nts to

bject or

es, have a

s. Invite

Stump

ns that

ꙮ Individual Timelines
SP–23 ☉

In September, give each student a timeline that you have prepared for the school year and divided into months. These can be kept on a bulletin board or inside a manila folder. Provide room for students to write their accomplishments, record their birthdays, add special events such as field trips and the arrival of new siblings, and other news. When students have personal experience creating and reading timelines, they will be better prepared to read and respond to them when they encounter them on high-stakes tests and in other academic situations.

❧ Story Planning Pyramid
SP-24 👁

To help struggling writers build a framework for their writing, use a planning pyramid. See the reproducible Story Planning Pyramid on page 192 for a simple organizer students can use when they write.

❧ Cut-Ups
SP-25 👁

Use old *Ranger Rick, National Geographic,* or other magazines for this motivating writing activity. Find several pictures of different kinds of animals. Cut each picture into several parts and mix the pieces to create new creatures. Then make several photocopies of each new animal because children will want to do more than one. Place these in a writing center and have students write sentences about the new creature.

They should include the following information:

> What is the creature's name?
>
> Where does it live?
>
> What does it like to eat?
>
> What sort of noise does it make?

If you are studying animals in a science unit, add questions that use new vocabulary, such as:

> Does this animal migrate?
>
> Does it hibernate?
>
> What special adaptations for protecting itself does it have?

Mechanics

Sticky Punctuation
ME-1 👁

When children have trouble remembering to add punctuation to their writing, try this strategy. Buy a package of round, colorful sticky dots at a dollar store—the kind you'd use for marking items at a yard sale. Use a fine-point black marker to draw the various kinds of punctuation marks that you expect the student to be able to use, one mark on a dot. Then when he is writing, have him peel off a sticky dot with the right punctuation mark for the sentence he has written and stick it where it should go. He must reread the sentence and consider his choices to do this.

TIP

When you have a student who forgets to start a new sentence with a capital letter, let him use a highlighter to highlight all the end punctuation in his writing. Then have him start editing at the beginning of this piece. Every time he sees highlighting, it's a cue that his next letter must be a capital letter.

Live Punctuation
ME-2

Write a sentence to review in big letters on the chalkboard or marker board. Have several children each wear a different sign with one of the punctuation marks you are teaching drawn on it in wide black marker. Use an apostrophe, a comma, a period, a question mark, an exclamation mark, and quotation marks. The children bring the sentence to life by standing in front of it in the right places. Another child reads the sentence using the punctuation to make it fluent. Repeat this process with other sentences so that everyone in the group gets a turn to be a punctuation mark and children get to see all the different kinds of punctuation marks in action.

Circle Spelling
ME–3

When a student has trouble encoding the words he wants to use in a story, teach him to write as many of the letters as he can according to the sounds he hears in the word. Next, have him circle the word and just keep writing. Reassure him that when you conference with him about his writing, there will be time to look at the circled words and decide on each one's conventional spelling.

Reversals
ME–4

To help students who reverse words when they write, place a green sticky dot on the left-hand side of the paper and a red one on the right-hand side to cue students where to start and stop.

TIP

Remind students to skip lines as they write so they have room to add and revise. For those who have trouble remembering, prepare lined paper that has every other line highlighted.

Revising and Editing

Don't Leave Home Without Them!
RE-1

Give students these visual cues for editing and revising their writing. Make a large poster to display with the following cues on it and copy it for students' writing folders. Add pictures of a brain, hands, fingers, eyes, ears, and mouth for your visual learners. Before the students begin to write, have them review this cueing system. Remind them to look at it again when they tell you they are done or are ready for a writing conference.

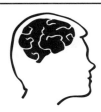

Brain

Use your brain to think about what you will write. Make pictures in your mind of what you might write about.

Hands

Use your hands and fingers to draw a web or sketch of your ideas and start writing. Skip lines.

Eyes

Use your eyes to look carefully at what you wrote. Did you use punctuation marks? Did you use capitals?

Ears

Use your ears to hear what you wrote. Touch each word as you say it. Did you leave any words out? Does your writing make sense?

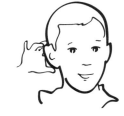

Mouth

Use your mouth to read the story to a friend to make sure it makes sense. Writing should sound like talk written down.

129

Write with the 5 Ws + H
RE-2

When a student has trouble adding simple details to fill out a sentence, teach him this technique. After he finishes writing, he looks at his work to see if he has included a *who*, *what*, *where*, *when*, *why*, and *how*. Do this with your student several times and then give him a written reminder to keep in his writing folder. See the example below for how you would walk your student through this revising technique. Be prepared to do it numerous times for some reluctant writers.

The man left.
   (What man or which man?)
The tall man left.
   (Where did he leave? Where was he?)
The tall man left the movie.
   (Why did he leave the movie?)
The tall man left the movie because his cell phone was ringing.
   (When did he leave?)
Halfway through the movie, the tall man left because his cell phone was ringing.
   (How did he leave?)
The tall man quickly left halfway through the movie because his cell phone was ringing.

Pair and Share
RE-3

Pair students to share their writing. Each one listens to his partner's work, then tells him one thing he liked about the story and asks one question he has about it. After they share, students must respond to their partner's question by adding to or clarifying their writing.

MATH

Number Recognition and Number Sense (NR)

Math Facts (MF)

Place Value (PV)

Operations (OP)

Fractions and Decimals (FD)

Time, Money, and Measurement (TM)

Word Problems (WP)

Geometry (GE)

General Strategies for Math Success

- Provide reference posters that give your visual learners cues (+ means add, – means subtract, etc.)

- Use sandpaper numbers on flash cards to help children who have reversals and to aid tactile-kinesthetic learners.

- Let students use mini chalkboards or marker boards in place of paper and pencil.

- Give students practice turning math facts into word problems.

- Highlight or color code operational words and symbols in directions and word problems to reduce confusion (orange for addition, yellow for subtraction).

- Group problems by similarities in wording and operation. When the type of problem changes, draw a heavy black line or use a Wikki Stix to give students a heads up.

- Draw circles or boxes around problems with similar operations.

- If the operations change at the end of each row or at the end of a page, draw a small stop sign at the end of the row or at the bottom of the page.

- Cut work sheets into strips to avoid overwhelming students. When they finish one strip, then give them another if they need more practice. Also, decrease the number of problems you assign. If you can determine that the student understands the operation or algorithm based on 8 problems, don't give her 16 to do.

- Arrange problems from easiest to hardest and separate them with a dark line.

- Use Wikki Stix to outline the problems you want the student to fix, or let her use them to choose which problems she wants to do on a page. You can say, "There are 20 problems on this page. Choose 3 from each row that you want to do."

- Provide answer banks at the top or bottom of a page.

- Let students check completed work using a calculator. Similarly, have them do half of the problems independently and the other half with a calculator.

- Reinforce odd and even number recognition by having students do only the even-numbered or odd-numbered problems on a page or a work sheet.

- Provide a variety of manipulatives to help children build understanding and achieve success. The kind of manipulative that "clicks" for one child might not do it for another child.

- Let students work with a buddy so that they can talk through the steps needed to solve a problem. This is especially helpful to auditory learners.

- Use 1-inch square graph paper for young students to organize their numbers and centimeter graph paper for older students. Similarly, have students turn lined paper horizontally for arranging problems with multiple digits. This is especially helpful when students need to regroup for addition and subtraction. (See illustration.)

$$
\begin{array}{r} 443 \\ -121 \\ \hline \end{array}
\qquad
\begin{array}{r} 639 \\ -425 \\ \hline \end{array}
\qquad
\begin{array}{r} 301 \\ -236 \\ \hline \end{array}
$$

Number Recognition and Number Sense

Screen Boards
NR–1

Use a 12 x 18-inch piece of plywood or the bottom of a soda case for this strategy. Cover the left half with acetate or a piece of old lamination. Make sure the left-hand edge isn't taped down, since this is where a piece of paper will be slipped under. Cover the other side of the board with screening or rug canvas. This piece gets taped to the piece of lamination. Place a correct model of a numeral, letter, or word underneath the lamination. Have the student trace over the model with a wipe-off pen. Next, she traces on a piece of paper placed over the screen. If she uses a thick crayon, the numeral or letter will have a raised effect for future tracing. Students can also use the screen board to reinforce correct spelling and review sight words. Three tracings in a row will help reinforce information.

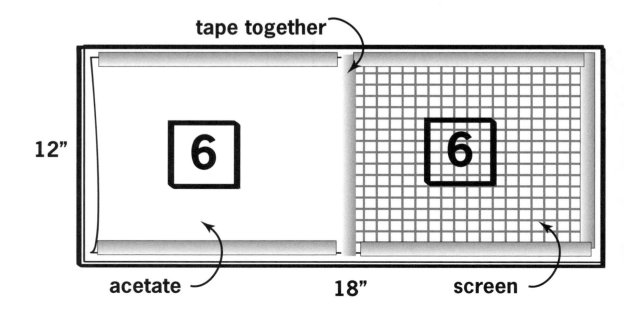

⚓ Canvas Charts
NR-2 ◪

To help students learn to form numerals correctly, let them trace numerals over needlepoint or rug canvas. A correct model of the numeral can be placed underneath the canvas while the student traces on top with an index finger. Students can place a piece of white paper over the canvas and use crayons to trace numerals on the paper. Make sure they have a model to copy. The raised effect made with crayons on white paper over the canvas offers a lasting tactile impression for students. They can also practice letter, word, and phrase formation this way.

⚓ Water Painting
NR-3 ◪

Provide 3-inch paintbrushes and small buckets of water. Students paint large numerals or letters on the chalkboard or playground and have peers check their work. This is also a fun way for them to practice writing letters, sight words, or spelling words.

TIP

For more ways to help children recognize and write numerals correctly, see the phonics section. Many of the strategies for helping young learners to recognize and write alphabet letters can also be used with numbers.

In a Row
NR-4 👁

Create a set of index cards with words representing the ordinal numbers *first* through *fifteenth* on them. Use each word several times. Deal three cards to each child and have them examine their cards and put them in order from smallest to largest. If a student has three cards in consecutive order, for example, *first, second,* and *third,* the student places the cards face up on the table and "goes out." If a student does not have three consecutive numbers, she draws a card from the deck. If she can use that number, she keeps it and discards another card. The goal is to get three cards in consecutive order and exit the game.

You can use this same game with students who need to review the sequence of letters in the alphabet.

Odd and Even
NR-5 👁 ⬕

To help a student understand odd and even numbers, give her a visual cue. Ten cubes, popsicle sticks, or other items will help build understanding. Teach her that for even numbers, each item will be able to "partner up" with another. Thus, for the number 4, she takes four cubes and pairs two and two. For the number 7, she will be able to make three sets of partners, but one cube will not have a partner and will be "the odd man out." When she has built understanding this way, show her how to look at the number in the ones place of a two-digit, three-digit, or four-digit number. If the number is 1, 3, 5, 7, or 9, then the entire number is an odd number. If the number in the ones place is 0, 2, 4, 6, or 8, the entire number, regardless of how many digits it has, will be an even number.

Number Line Guess
NR-6 ◖

Distribute a number line that goes from 1 to 20 to each child. Assign one student to be "it." Give the student a number. Ask her to describe to the class where her number falls on the number line without saying what the number is. For example, "I have a number that is greater than 4," "This number is six hops to the right of 3," or "The number is two hops to the left of 11." "What is the number?" Students take turns describing numbers using the number line.

Change this activity to Letter Guess. Give students an alphabet strip and tell the student who is "it" what her letter is. For example, if it's *o*, she may say, "My letter comes after *m* and before *p*."

Skip Counting
NR-7 ⬕ 👁 ◖

Give children plenty of opportunities and lots of different ways to practice skip counting. When they line up for recess, have them find a partner. Each pair counts by two, so the first pair in line says "two," and the second pair says, "four" and so on. Do the same thing to practice counting by threes, fours, and fives.

Whenever you ask students to count, show them how to do it by grouping items. If you've played a concentration match game and you are determining which child has the most cards, don't let them count cards one by one. Instead, have them count by twos.

For visual learners, provide a 100 chart and let them use crayons to color in the numbers they say when they count by fours, fives, sixes, and so on.

'Gator Than and Less Than
NR-8 👁

Try this strategy for students who have trouble remembering how to read the symbols for greater than (>) and less than (<). Write two numbers on the board, leaving plenty of space between them. Draw a gaping

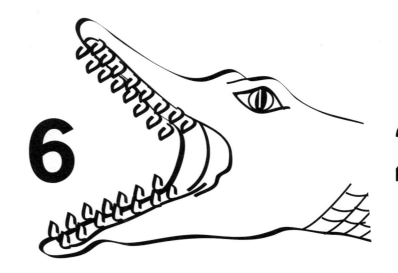

alligator mouth between the two numbers but open and pointing to the larger number. Tell children that a hungry alligator always eats the larger number.

A different strategy that works better for some students and works especially well when only one number is used is to demonstrate to your students that the symbol for less than (<) looks a bit like a letter *l* that got caught in a vise and squeezed. When they see the squished *l*, they should remember that the word *less* begins with an *l* and the symbol < means *less than*. It's wise to teach students both of these strategies since on a formal assessment, a question may not ask students to compare two numbers. For example, < 10 of the students in our class are boys.

Math Facts

Twister Math
MF-1

Use an inexpensive
shower curtain
liner, an old table-
cloth or sheet, or
a Twister mat from a game you buy at a yard sale. Cover the game board with
numbers for children to review. Differentiate this activity by changing the directions for the children you are working with, so for some, the direction card may
say, "Put a foot on 3 and a hand on 7." Other students might be directed to place
their right foot on 3 and their left hand on 9 and multiply the numbers.

Vary this popular game for language arts. You can create cards that ask students
to place one hand on an adjective and another on a verb or a compound word, or
to put their right hand on a 2-syllable word and their left foot on a 3-syllable word.

Musical Math Chairs
MF-2

Play this game just like musical chairs to get students up and moving so that
their brains get oxygenated, they get to exercise, and they practice material that
needs to be reviewed or reinforced. The difference is that on each seat, you will
have placed a laminated card with a math problem on it. When the music stops
and students claim a seat, they can remain in that seat only if they can complete
the problem on the card within a time limit that you set.

This works great for language arts, too. Students can review vocabulary, rhymes,
initial or final letter phonemes, blends, or just about anything else you can think of.

⚓ Math Fact Search
MF-3 👁

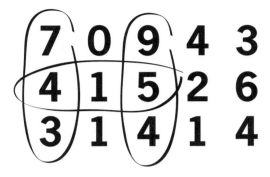

Create a word search format that uses numbers instead of letters. The student's job is to find and circle three numbers that form a math fact family either vertically, horizontally, or diagonally. Start with number searches using only one operation, such as addition. As the students' skill levels increase, include different operations in your search. Have the students identify the operations they recognize as they circle fact families.

Beach Ball Fun
MF-4 🗲

Use a large, segmented beach ball to help students "catch" their facts. Write a numeral on each segment in permanent marker. Before you toss the ball to a student, state the operation to use, such as subtraction. When he catches the ball, he must subtract the two numbers under his thumbs. This is also useful for number recognition.

To use this with language arts, write words on each segment of the ball for students to define or write phrases in the segments that students must read fluently. They can generate a rhyming word for the words under their thumbs, a word that starts or ends the same, has the same number of syllables, and so on. This activity is limited only by your imagination.

MATH FLUENCY

Just as knowing many words helps children to be fluent and effective readers, knowing number facts allows students to compute faster and more accurately. There are lots of motivating and enjoyable ways for students to practice math facts. These work better than tiresome drills that children dislike and would prefer to avoid. Try some of the ones in this section, but also look at other sections of this book for language-based games and strategies that can be adapted for math fact practice.

⚓ Math Fact Stampede
MF-5 🖼 👁

Provide the student with a 3 x 12-inch sentence strip or oak tag strip, plus a variety of rubber stamps and stamp pads. The child chooses a math fact flash card from a set and illustrates the problem using the sentence strip and stamps.

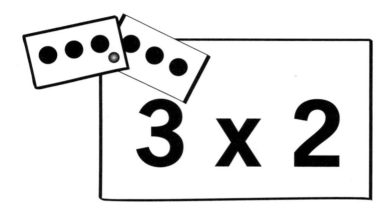

Flipping Facts
MF-6 🖼 👁

Flipping flash cards help students to learn multiplication facts. Use index cards and brass brads. If a student is having trouble with 3 x 2, for example, design a card that looks like the one in the illustration.

⚓ Mailing Facts
MF-7 🖼

Get 20 white envelopes and write a number from 1 to 20 on each one. Designate one student as the mail carrier. Give the student a set of index cards with addition and subtraction math facts that result in answers from 1 to 20. The mail carrier's task is to correctly deliver the index cards to the right envelopes. Provide an answer key that the student can use to check his work when he is finished or let him use a calculator to check the facts on the cards that he has placed in each envelope.

⚓ Pocket Math
MF-8 🖼

Glue 10 library card pockets on oak tag and write the numerals 1 to 10 on them, one number per pocket. Write math facts on index cards and let students match the cards to the correct pocket. Write the answers on the backs of the cards to make this a self-checking strategy.

Butterfly Facts
MF-9

Have the student trace around each of his feet. Write his name on each foot and laminate the feet. Next draw an outline of a butterfly and laminate the outline. On the center of the butterfly's body, write a number for review. Have students use an erasable crayon or marker and write math facts on each of their foot tracings that result in the number on the butterfly's body. Have them place their "math feet" on each side of the butterfly's body for wings.

The butterfly can also be used for letter and sound review. Write the letter to be reviewed on the butterfly's body and have students either write words or draw pictures that begin or end with the letter on the body. For rhyming, use a sticker or a rubber stamp to make a picture on the body and ask students to draw pictures of things that rhyme on each wing. For initial or final sound fluency, do the same thing but change the directions. If you put a sticker of a horse on the body, students would draw a hat on one wing and a house on the other, for example.

Inside-Outside Fact Review
MF-10

Have the students stand in two circles, one inside the other. Make sure each circle has the same number of students; if you have an odd number of students, you or an aide can stand opposite the unpaired student. Have each student in the inside circle turn to face the child nearest her in the outer circle. The child in the inner circle gives the child who is facing her a review problem to answer. Now have the "outers" move two steps to the right; the "inners" give their new partners another review problem. This continues until all the children in the inner circle have worked with all the children in the outer circle. Then have the two sets of students switch places so that the outer-circle children become the inner circle.

This game is also fun to use when reviewing sight words, spelling words, states and capitals, and many other facts. Try it with vocabulary words where one partner reads the meaning and the other has to guess the word, then reverse the process.

❧ Flower Power
MF–11 👁

Cut out a 4-inch circle for the center of the flower. Write a number on it. Have students attach petals of math facts that result in the number in the center.

This can also be used for letter and sound fluency if you write a letter such as *b* in the center and ask children to glue pictures from magazines or draw their own pictures on each petal that begin with the same sound.

❧ Stick to the Facts
MF–12 ❧

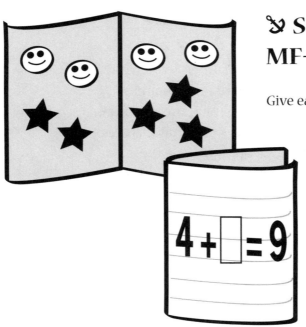

Give each student a page or two of small peel-off stickers, plus a few blank 5 x 8-inch index cards. Instruct students to fold the cards in half, open them up, and apply a random number of stickers to the left and right sides of the card. Tell them that the total number of stickers on both sides of the card cannot be greater than 18. Have the students fold their cards in half with the stickers on the inside. On the front outside flap, have each student write a math problem based on the stickers inside, such as 4 + ? = 9. Laminate the cards and have students pass them around for other students to solve.

❧ Dog-Gone Good Facts
MF–13

Use a cutout of a puppy (see p. 174). Make copies and laminate them. Write a math problem to be solved on each dog's body and leave a blank space for the answer. Add an orange mini sticky note cut to look like a dog's tongue and hide the answer under it so the student can check his work and get immediate feedback. Have the student write his answer in the appropriate space with an erasable marker or crayon.

Fishy Fact Families
MF-14 👁

Cut out the head and tail of a fish body and write the same number on each piece. Have students create fish scales from index cards or colorful construction paper and write math facts that result in the number written on the head and tail of the fish. Use the reproducible on page 172 for this activity if you wish.

Number Bear, Number Bear
MF-15 🔊

Using a familiar chant from children's literature, teach students math facts by having them chant "10 Bear, 10 Bear, what do you see?" "I see 7 + 3 equal to me." To add a visual component, have students create bears and matching number fact families (see the illustration).

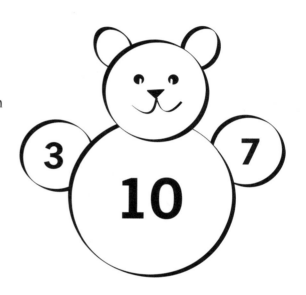

This strategy is also helpful for phonics practice and word families. If the word to be rhymed is *mat*, your chant might be "Rhyming Bear, Rhyming Bear, what do you see?" "I see cat and hat rhyming with me."

Hang Ups
MF-16 📷

Give small groups of students a plastic clothes hanger and pinch clothespins. Have the students choose a number of clothespins and hook them to the hanger. Ask one student in each group to write the number of clothespins on the hanger on a piece of paper. Then have another student move a random number of clothespins to the right side of the hanger. Ask another student to write that number and provide an operational sign. The next student writes the number of clothespins that results. (They need to provide the equal sign.) Have students explore how many other ways they can move the clothespins and use the numbers in different number sentences. Have them record each number sentence they create.

7-Up Facts
MF–17 ✍

Turn the game of 7-Up into a fact review. Choose seven students to come to the front of the class. Give each one an index card with a math problem written on it. Have the rest of the students put their heads down on their desks and raise one thumb. Each of the seven students will tap a friend by pressing her thumb down and handing the friend her card. When all seven students have given away their cards and returned to the front of the room, say "Heads up, 7 Up." The students holding the index cards stand. Next you call out an answer. The student who has the problem that matches that answer has a chance to guess who gave it to her. If she guesses correctly, she switches places with that child.

This game also can be used for spelling and vocabulary review.

Moving Math Facts
MF–18 ✍

Write an addition fact to be completed on a piece of paper and give the student counters, beans, or other manipulatives to place directly next to each addend. Have her move the counters to the answer spot. Moving the manipulatives reinforces understanding of combining sets to add. Use the same strategy with subtraction.

Desk Number Lines
MF–19 👁

All students may need to use a desk number line at some time. Often parents ask how to use the number line for addition, so a line that can be carried home and back to school is helpful. Or show parents how to use a simple ruler as a number line to solve easy math fact problems. Teach students how to look at simple problems such as 4 + 5. They place a finger on the first number in the problem and then hop forward 5 more to get the answer. Do the reverse for subtraction. For 10 – 2, students start at the first number and hop backward 2 places to land on the number 8.

Playing for Face Value
MF-20 ■

Use a deck of regular playing cards. Post the rules for the face value of each card as follows:

Any card with a face	=	1
Aces	=	0
All red numbers	=	add that face value
All black numbers	=	subtract that face value

Deal five cards to each player. The players must examine their cards and decide whether they can create a number sentence with the cards they have.

For instance:

Jack		**Queen**		**Ace**		**5 (Diamonds)**		**6 (Clubs)**		
(1	+	1	+	0	+	5)	–	6	=	1

The student with the highest score for each hand wins a "funny buck" (see p. 169) which can be cashed in for a reward of your choice, such as extra computer time or a homework pass, at the end of the game.

RULES

QUEEN = 1

ACE = 0

THREE = +

THREE = -

8-4+6+0+1=11

Spin the Bottle
MF-21

Write a number with an operational sign on a plastic half-gallon tea or juice bottle (for instance, + 5). Distribute number cards to the students. Have a child spin the bottle. When the bottle stops spinning and points to a particular child, that child will solve the math problem using the + 5 and the number on her card. A child with a card with 12 on it would answer 17. If she's right, her classmates give her the thumbs-up sign, and she spins the bottle. If she's unsure, she asks her classmates for help.

For vocabulary review, write a word on the bottle, spin it, and whoever it points to gives the meaning in his own words.

The Family Tree
MF-22

Use a cutout of a tree for this activity. On the trunk of the tree, write three numbers to make a fact family. For example, write 3, 7, and 10. Instruct the students to write a different math fact on each branch of the tree to illustrate that fact family.

Guess If You Can
MF-23

Place cards with the numbers 1 to 19 written on them in a shoe box or hat. Designate one student to be "it." Have the student choose two cards from the hat or box. He must describe the two numbers by giving the result of a math fact. For example, if the student chooses 15 and 9, he gives the other students clues by saying, "I have two numbers whose difference is 6." A child called upon to respond might ask, "Do you have 9 and 3?" The student who drew the cards says "No" and writes that guess, 9 – 3, on the board. The child who is "it" continues to call on students until someone guesses correctly. Then that student chooses the next two cards from the hat or box.

Finger Clues for Counting On
MF-24

When children have a difficult time doing math facts without counting on their fingers (and toes!), give them a strategy that is more efficient and helps them to arrive at the correct answer. Give a child a problem such as 9 + 3. Write it on paper and draw a line through the first number, 9, and have the child place 3 fingers in the air. Show her how to start counting those fingers with the number after 9, putting down each finger as she counts 10, 11, and 12. When the child has no more fingers left up, the last number she has said is the answer.

Headband Facts
MF-25

If head lice are not a concern, use inexpensive terry sweat-bands for this activity. Students work in pairs. They put on headbands and you place an index card with a numeral on it in each of their bands. They face each other so that they can see their partner's number but not their own. You call out a sum of the two numbers and each child tries to figure out what number is in her own band. The first one to guess correctly wins the round.

TIP

Help students learn to space their math problems on a sheet of paper with this trick. Place a plastic six-pack can holder over a blank piece of paper. Teach the student to place one math problem inside each can ring. (The need to use this cueing system will soon disappear.) Use this for letting students organize spelling words, vocabulary, and word families, too.

Easy Doubles
MF-26

When you teach math facts, start with the doubles. Most children find that it is easier to learn the sums for "doubles" such as 6 + 6, 7 + 7, 8 + 8, than it is to remember 5 + 6, 7 + 8, 8 + 9, etc. Once they have mastered the doubles and can give you the answers with automaticity, you can show them how easy it is to add 1 or 2 to the more troublesome facts (7 + 8, 9 + 7). Use the same strategy with subtraction. Students who have mastered 7 + 7 = 14 will be able to figure out 14 - 7 easily. As they gain confidence, they should be able to mentally manipulate numbers for more difficult subtraction facts. If they know that 16 - 8 = 8, then for 16 - 9, they will shift 1 from an 8 to come up with the answer of 7.

Place Value

Number, Number, What Can It Be?
PV-1 [C]

Choose one student to be "it." Write a number on a piece of oak tag. Hold the card behind the student's back so the class can see it and ask the class to give the student hints about the number; for instance:

"It's bigger than 20, but less than 30."

"It's an odd number."

"It's divisible by 3."

The student tries to guess the correct number in as few clues as possible.

Use the same game to review vocabulary. Write a new word on the oak tag, hold it behind the student's back, and invite the class to give him synonyms or definitions that will help him to guess the word. You can even play Genre, Genre, What Can It Be? Write *fairy tale* on the card, for example, and have students give hints such as *dragon, castle, once upon a time*, and so on.

Place Value Puzzles
PV-2

Create puzzles out of oak tag or construction paper, using seasonal shapes (snowmen, leaves, turkeys, etc.). Cut each shape in half, write a number on one half, and describe the number by place values on the other half. Students match the pieces and read the numbers to reinforce understanding of place value.

You can use the same idea for vocabulary words and definitions, initial letter sounds and pictures, number of phonemes in a word, and more.

Who's in Place?
PV–3 ◼

Give students cards with the numerals 0 through 9 written on them. On three large sheets of butcher paper or poster board, write the words *hundreds, tens,* and *ones*. Place these on the floor and then call out a number, such as 342. The child holding a 3 stands on the hundreds sheet, the child with 4 stands on the tens sheet, and the child who has 2 stands on the ones sheet. With the same three children, switch the number to 432 and have them form this number to further assess understanding of place value.

You can also use this idea with younger learners for language arts. Give them cards with letters for sounds you are reinforcing. To practice CVC words, say the word *bat* and see if the children holding the *b, a,* and *t* can place themselves in the correct letter sequence, then ask them to make the word *tab*. Check to be sure they are arranging the letters so that the word is read from left to right.

Read My Mind
PV–4 ◼ ◉

Work on place value and cleaning desk tops at the same time! Cover tables or desks with unscented shaving cream. Tell students they are going to try to read your mind. Describe a number and ask students to write it in their shaving cream. For example, say, "I am thinking of a number that has 7 hundreds, 5 tens, and 6 ones. Write my number if you can read my mind." For older students, mix up the values and ask for the number that has 8 tens, 5 hundreds, and no ones. You can vary this by having children use Play-Doh or letting them write a number in pudding, dry Jell-O, sand, salt, or on finger-paint bags (see p. 42).

To make this a language arts activity, have students write the word you are thinking of when you say, "I'm thinking of the letters *t, u,* and *b*. Write the word if you can read my mind." This strategy is also useful for children who have reversal issues for numbers, letters, or words.

TIP

Another good way to reinforce the concept of place value is with decks of I am, who is cards (also called I have, who has). You can learn more about this game and see examples at www.mathwire.com/whohas/whohas.html.

"46"

Bean Stalks
PV–5

Let students help assemble the materials for this activity before they use it to build conceptual understanding.

1. Glue 10 dried beans (or use rigatoni) to a Popsicle stick. Each child makes at least ten of these Popsicle sticks with ten beans on each.

2. Place the sticks in an empty coffee can or juice can.

3. Place a cup of loose beans in each work area.

When reviewing place value, write a number on the board, such as 46. Have each student use the sticks (4) and the loose beans (6) to demonstrate tens and ones.

Place Value Race
PV–6

Make two sets of cards numbered 0 through 9 on 9 x 12-inch oak-tag sheets. Then divide your class into two teams. Each team will need a set of cards. Give one card to each student. If you have more than 20 students, the extra students can be scorekeepers, timekeepers, and coaches. (Rotate roles so these students get a chance to play.)

Explain to students that you will say a number, count to 3, and then say "go." Each team tries to be the first to correctly form your number in the front of the room. If you say "2,308" the students on each team with a 2, a 3, a 0, and an 8 card will race to the front and arrange themselves in the correct order.

Flipping for Places
PV-7 ◣

Divide students into groups of four and give each group nine tiddlywinks and a 12 x 18-inch piece of oak tag divided into thirds and labeled *hundreds, tens,* and *ones.* One child flips the nine tiddlywinks, which should fall in either the hundreds, tens, or ones place. A second child calls out the number that results. Another child writes the corresponding number and the fourth checks the response and clears the board. Children rotate roles for subsequent turns.

⚓ Ring It
PV-8 ◣ 👁

Using the plastic spirals that come with a bookbinding machine, hook together three different colored index cards. You can also use metal ring binders on a wooden dowel. Number each set of cards 0 through 9. Call out a number such as 789, and have the children flip their individual cards to form that number. For an anchor activity, record the numbers on a sheet of paper beforehand and have children do this at a learning center. Have them record the number they create each time so that you can assess understanding later.

This also works well with letters and sounds. Say a word and have students flip letter cards to form that word correctly.

Operations

First Numeral
OP–1

Ask students who are not yet able to complete long division problems to solve only the first, or first and second, numerals in the quotient. Given the problem 81,453 divided by 9, some may solve only 81 divided by 9 and then stop. As they become more confident, they will work toward solving the complete problem.

Cheeseburger Division
OP–2 👁

To help them remember the steps in long division, teach students the following cueing aid: Does McDonald's Sell Cheese Burgers? Write this question on a poster and highlight D for divide, M for multiply, S for subtract, C for compare, and B for bring down.

⚓ My Own Multiplication
OP–3 🖾

Give students a handful of rubber bands or yarn. After a quiz or other assessment, have them decide which multiplication facts they need to review. Glue rubber bands or yarn on paper to create circles for number sets. If a student needs to practice 7 x 3, she creates either 7 or 3 sets on her paper. For fun homework or class work, have students glue objects inside the loops to represent multiplication facts. The student who made 3 loops on her paper will glue 7 beans or other small objects inside each loop to practice the math fact 3 x 7 = 21.

Multiplication Charts
OP–4 👁 ✒

Have multiplication charts made out of sturdy oak tag ready for students who choose to use them. Demonstrate how they can use rubber bands or yarn to keep their place on the chart and find the product where two factors intersect. See page 193 for a reproducible multiplication chart.

Finger Multiplication for the 9s
OP–5 ✒

Share with students this strategy to use when one of the factors in a multiplication problem is 9. Have them place both of their hands on their desks. Teach them to always start counting with the pinky on their left hand. If the problem is 3 x 9, have them start counting on their left-hand pinky and count to 3. The finger that is counted as 3 is folded down. Now the product is right at their fingertips. The fingers to the left of the folded finger are counted as tens (there are two of these) and the fingers to the right of the folded finger are counted as ones (there are seven of these). The answer is 27. Children love tricks and short-cuts. Be sure to remind them that they always begin counting on their left-hand pinky and the number to count is the factor that is not 9.

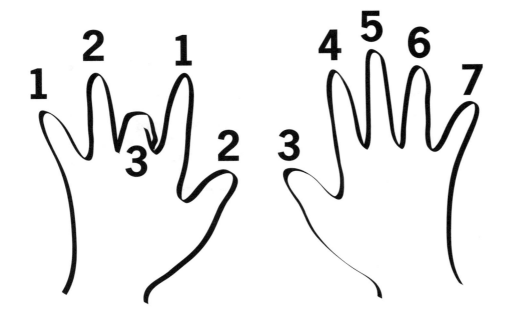

Concentration Math
OP-6 ◣

Play this game just like the old TV show. Use 20 index cards. Depending on the concept students need to work on, make card pairs like math facts and answers, geometric shapes and their names, or vocabulary words and definitions. The possibilities are almost endless. Randomly mix the cards and arrange face down, four cards in five rows. Students turn two cards over at a time and attempt to match the cards. Color code cards by using one color of cards for the problems and a different color for the answers. If you send home the cards and a list of facts, vocabulary, or other material to reinforce, many parents will be happy to do the writing for you at home.

Math Map
OP-7 ◉

To help children recall the necessary steps in doing math problems, provide them with a map they can use as a visual organizer. Laminate a desk-top map for each student and encourage students to check off each step as they complete it.

Math Map

1. **Compare two numbers.**

2. **Circle the greater number.**

3. **Say that number.**

4. **Now count onward.**

5. **Write the answer.**

$4 + 3$

$\textcircled{4} + 3$

"four"

"five, six, seven"

"7"

Fractions and Decimals

Fraction Number Lines
FD-1 👁

Fraction number lines are helpful for children who can't visualize part to whole. Keep these on the students' desks to use as needed.

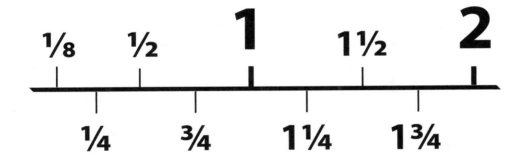

Fraction Cakes
FD-2 👁 ✴

Give each student a piece of brown construction or butcher paper that is 8 x 10 inches. Practice dividing the cake in half, in fourths, and then in eighths. Have students decorate 3/8 of their cake with "sprinkles" (glitter), put stars on 1/4 of their cake, and so on.

Fraction Action
FD-3

Use the Simon Says format to review fractions and to introduce decimals. Say "Simon says show me 3/10 of your fingers." Students should hold up three fingers. If you say, "Show me 1/10," they should not hold any fingers up, since you didn't say "Simon says." If you say, "Simon says show me 5/10 of your fingers," students should show you five fingers. Have them do this with one hand and then begin a discussion about fraction equivalents. They should see that 5 out of 10 fingers equals half of their fingers, or one hand.

Easy-Does-It Decimals
FD-4

Decimals are much less daunting for young learners when you relate them to something the children already understand. Use money to explain tenths and hundredths. Relating dimes to tenths and pennies to hundredths allows students to use prior knowledge and make a connection to the new math to come. Using a 10-by-10 grid is a good pictorial representation of decimals for visual learners. See page 194 for a reproducible you can use. When you show them that .03 is the same as 3 of the 100 boxes shaded in, decimals are easier to understand. For .1 students shade in 10 out of the 100 boxes.

CONNECTING THE NEW AND THE KNOWN

When you start to explore fractions, be sure to remind students of everything they already know about these special numbers. For example, they know that a half hour is 1/2 of an hour and that fifty cents is equal to 1/2 of a dollar. Some students will know that four quarters make a whole dollar and that 15 minutes is the same as 1/4 of an hour.

Time, Money, and Measurement

⚓ Dining Out
TM-1 🔳

Ask each student to bring a restaurant menu to school, and then give out individual resealable plastic bags of play money. Each student fills out an order form listing all the food items he can buy from his menu with the amount of money in his plastic bag.

Double Coupons
TM-2 👁

Clip store coupons onto index cards, and write a monetary value for the featured product on the card below the coupon. Have students figure out what they would pay for the item if the coupon amount was worth double its face value.

Color-Coded Clocks
TM-3 👁

Color-code the clock hands throughout the school the same colors: yellow for the minute hand, blue for the hour hand. This helps students who are having trouble differentiating between the minute and hour hands to do so.

In the Money
TM-4 ⬛

Here's another way to play a money game. Make several sets of cards using coin stamps or ask a parent to do this for you. Be sure to make some cards that are the same amount but have different combinations of coins. For example, show a dollar with a card that has two quarters and five dimes and another card with three quarters, two dimes, and a nickel. Laminate the cards for durability.

Give pairs of students or small groups a deck of the money cards. Have one student in each group divide the cards evenly among the players. At the count of three, all players in the group put down a card with the coins facing up. Each student announces the value of the coins on his card and the one with the largest amount of money takes all the cards.

When two cards are shown that have the same monetary value, play Money War. The two cards can show different combinations of coins, as long as they total the same amount. Each player in the group puts down three cards, face down. Then they each put down another card face up. The player with the largest amount of money on his card takes all of the cards on the table at that point. To determine the winner, younger students can count their cards while older students might use calculators to determine who ended up with the most money.

Throwing Money Away
TM-5 ⬛

Make a picture of a trash can on a large piece of butcher paper or oak tag and place it on the floor. Tape a piece of masking tape on the floor three feet away from the picture. Have the children line up in two teams behind the tape.

Make two sets of cards with money values on them using money stamps (all under a dollar) to toss at the can. The object is for the students to toss the cards onto the can, and be the first team to throw a dollar away without going over that amount.

First and Last Hands
TM-6 👁

When teaching students how to discriminate between the hour hand and the minute hand, have each student write his first name on a color-coded hour hand. Have him write his last name on the minute hand. Attach the hands to a paper plate clock. Remind the student that he will always say his first name (hour) first and last name (minutes) last.

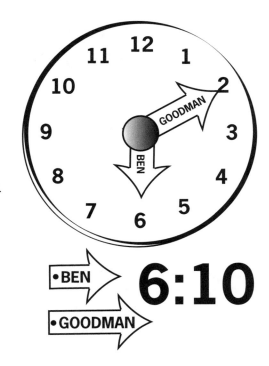

Making It Up
TM-7

Use a nonstandard form of measurement to help children understand the concept of measuring.

- Give them paper clips to measure how big their hands are.
- In March, give them paper shamrocks to measure their height.
- Let them use red Swedish fish to measure their desks.

Measurement Cues
TM-8 👁

To help children remember common measurements, use pictures. Create a picture of three sneakers in a front yard so they'll remember that there are 3 feet in a yard or use the handy reproducible on page 196. Mark each sneaker with a 12 for the number of inches in a foot.

For 4 quarts in a gallon, make a poster with a picture of a gallon milk jug or use the reproducible on page 197. Draw 4 quarts of milk on it. On each quart, make pictures of 4 cups so students remember that there are 4 cups in a quart.

Bubble Math
TM-9 ▧

Fill a dishpan with bubble solution. You can purchase a large container at a dollar store or make your own. Give students a straw and a paper cup filled halfway with bubble solution and place one plastic ruler for each student into the remaining bubble solution in the dishpan.

Have students spread about half of the solution out on their desks, being careful not to let any drip onto the floor. They should spread the solution out with their hands so that the whole surface of their desk is wet. Then have them dip the straw into the solution that is left in the cup and tilt it to touch the solution on their desks. Show them how to gently blow into the straw to blow a bubble. Next, show them how they can put a wet ruler into the top of a bubble to measure its height.

After students have practiced measuring height, have them measure a bubble that has popped by using the ruler to measure the diameter of the ring that remains. Caution: Remind students to keep their hands away from their eyes when they are using bubble solution and remind them not to inhale the bubble solution!

Word Problems

I've Got Problems!
WP-1

Let students make up their own word problems using information that relates to them. Give them either a format for writing problems or sentence stems. They can add information that is relevant to their lives and data to create word problems they can exchange with other students and solve.

Read-Aloud Problems
WP-2

Some students need to hear word problems read aloud in order to conceptualize the facts and the operations needed to solve them. Have students work in pairs or read a problem to themselves using a phonics phone.

Walking Through Problems
WP-3

Students who have trouble solving word problems are often more successful if they can act out the problem using manipulatives. If the problem involves giving something to another person or getting something, have students team up or work in small groups. You may be able to pair a student who is good in math but has trouble reading with a good reader who finds math to be a challenge. That means success for both of them.

Leveled Word Problems
WP-4

For some students who are good in math, it's the reading that interferes with them successfully solving word problems. Try this strategy to help these students to succeed. White out any unnecessary words or information that may slow down or confuse students. Use a highlighter or highlighting tape for key operational words, such as *how many more*. Read problems out loud to students and have them restate them in their own words.

How Many More?
WP-5 👁 🗲

Many children who are otherwise good mathematicians run into trouble when they see these three little words—"How many more?"—in a word problem. Use one-to-one correspondence to give them a visual representation for what's going on in these problems. For example, if the problem says that Mike has 8 plastic dinosaurs and Ted has 11, and asks the question "How many more does Ted have?" show the student how to use manipulatives to set up the problem. Let's say you use pennies to stand in for dinosaurs. Show the child how to make a column on her desk for Ted's dinos and another for Mike's dinos. Then she will use the pennies and give one to Ted and one to Mike repeatedly until Mike has 8. The problem tells her that Ted has 11, so she'll keep adding pennies to his column until she reaches that number. When she sees the one-to-one correspondence end, the difference is clear for her and so is the answer. Ted has 3 more than Mike.

Geometry

⚓ Shape Up
GE-1 👁

To help children become familiar with shapes, give them this activity. Have a variety of colorful shapes cut out of paper. Give children a math sheet with directions such as: Create a design using 3 triangles, 2 rectangles, a square and 4 circles. When you are happy with your design, glue it onto a sheet of blank paper. Have students label each shape with its correct name.

Find It
GE-2 👁 🖐

When you introduce geometric shapes, take students for a walk around the inside of your building or outside to the playground and have them try to find the shapes on the playground or on the building. Give visual learners a sheet with the shapes they should look for and the names of the shapes.

I Am, Who Is
GE-3 🗣

There are many ways to use the "I am, who is" or "I have, who has" game format. For geometry, create cards that describe shapes and angles. Your first card might say, "I am 2 short sides and 2 long sides. Who is 3 sides? The next card would say, "I am a triangle. Who is no straight lines?" To learn more about this activity and how to create cards, visit the following Web site: www.mathwire.com/whohas/whohas.html. There are even sample games to download.

Graph-a-Shape
GE-4 ▧

Combine shapes and graphs with this strategy that gets students up and moving. Use an inexpensive plastic shower-curtain liner or tablecloth to make this graph. On the bottom, draw a circle, a square, a rectangle, a triangle, and a rhombus. Have the children survey the room or the playground to find examples of these shapes. Set a time limit so that they are focused on the task at hand. When time is up, direct the students to return to the large graph and either place their object above the corresponding picture on the graph, or name their object that represents the shape. Use the data collected by students to discuss shapes and how frequently they occur.

REPRODUCIBLES

To get an idea of a child's preferred learning style, read each statement and ask him whether it describes him. Then tally how many A's (auditory), V's (visual), and T-K's (tactile-kinesthetic) you have circled.

Name_____ **Grade**____ **Date**_____ **Score**_____A ____V ____T-K

1. I like to stand up when I am doing a paper in school. (T-K)

2. I would rather listen to my teacher read a story than look at a book by myself. (A)

3. When a grown-up tells me something, I can usually remember what it was. (A)

4. I would rather draw a picture than play an outside game like kickball. (V)

5. It's easier to remember what my classmates look like than it is to remember their names. (V)

6. I don't like to read sitting at my desk. I'd rather lie on the rug or sit in a beanbag chair. (T-K)

7. When I write, I like to say the letters and the words to myself as I write them. (A)

8. My pencil point breaks a lot when I am writing. (T-K)

9. I can't concentrate if the TV is on. (A)

10. When I'm not sure how to spell a word, I write it in the air or on a piece of scrap paper to see if it looks right. (V)

11. When I read, I see the story in my head. (V)

12. When I read, I can hear the words I am reading in my head. (A)

13. When I am reading, I usually jiggle my foot or wiggle around in my seat. (T-K)

14. When I am trying to learn how to do something, I like to watch somebody else do it first. (V)

15. I like someone to tell me how to do something new. I listen to them and then I do it. (A)

16. I like to do things by myself until I get them right instead of watching someone else show me or tell me how to do them. (T-K)

17. I love to doodle and draw. (V)

18. I like to play a game or do a puzzle while I watch TV. (T-K)

19. My favorite class is: art (V) music (A) physical education (T-K)

20. To learn how a computer works I would: watch a movie about computers (V)
listen to someone explain how they work (A)
take a computer apart and see what I find out (T-K)

Name_____ Grade_____ Date_____

1. My favorite class in school is _____.

2. My three best friends are _____, _____, and _____.

3. I like to read books about _____.

4. I like to watch movies about _____.

5. My favorite Wii game or X cube game is _____.

6. I'd like my whole family to go to _____ for a month of vacation.

7. Two things I like to do after school are _____ and _____.

8. Two things I have to do after school are _____ and _____.

9. My favorite homemade food is _____.

10. My favorite take-out or eat-out food is _____.

11. I wish this teacher could teach me for the next 5 years. _____.

12. If I had a million dollars, I'd _____.

13. When I grow up, I could be a _____.

14. I think I know enough to invent _____.

15. My favorite thing to do outdoors is _____.

16. I think I watch about _____ hours of TV a day.

17. If I could change one thing about me, it would be _____.

18. The best thing about me is _____.

19. Something that people in this class don't know about me is _____

_____.

20. If I could change one thing about school it would be _____.

Team Meeting Review

DATE	RECOMMENDATION	NOTES
	☐ Continue with current intervention.	
Attendees Principal: Teacher: Others:	☐ Change frequency or duration of intervention to:	
	☐ Try new intervention:	
	☐ Change Tier to:	
	☐ Goals reached. Discontinue interventions.	
	Date of next meeting:	

Interventionist: _____   Initial Status _____

Target Area _____   Tier _____

Progress Monitoring Data

DATE	Intervention	Freq/Duration	Progress Monitoring Tool	Results/Observations

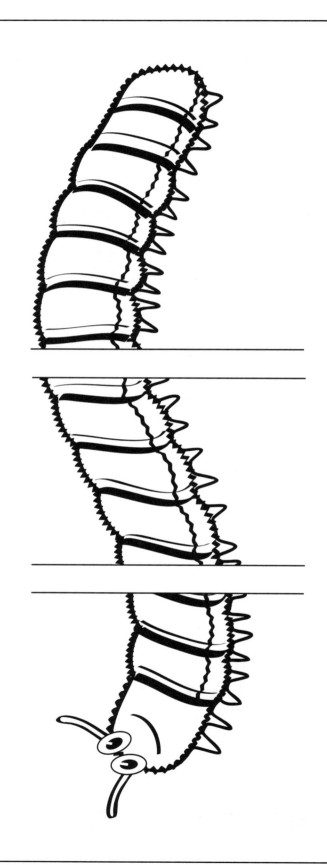

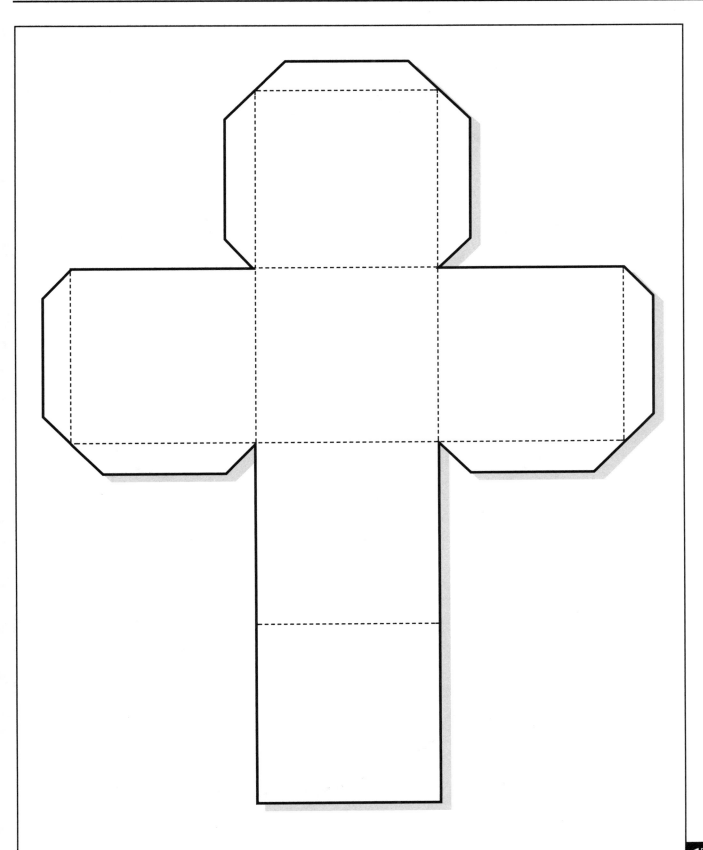

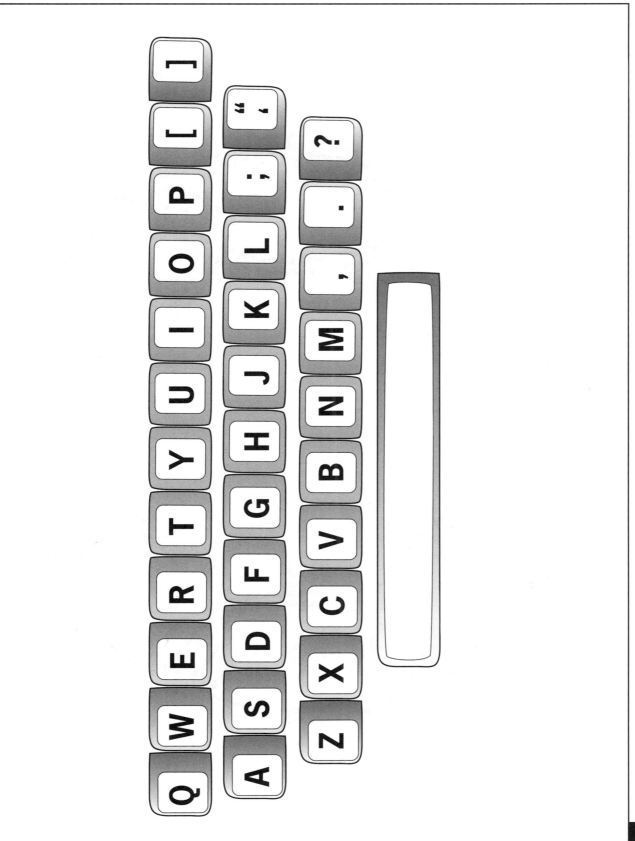

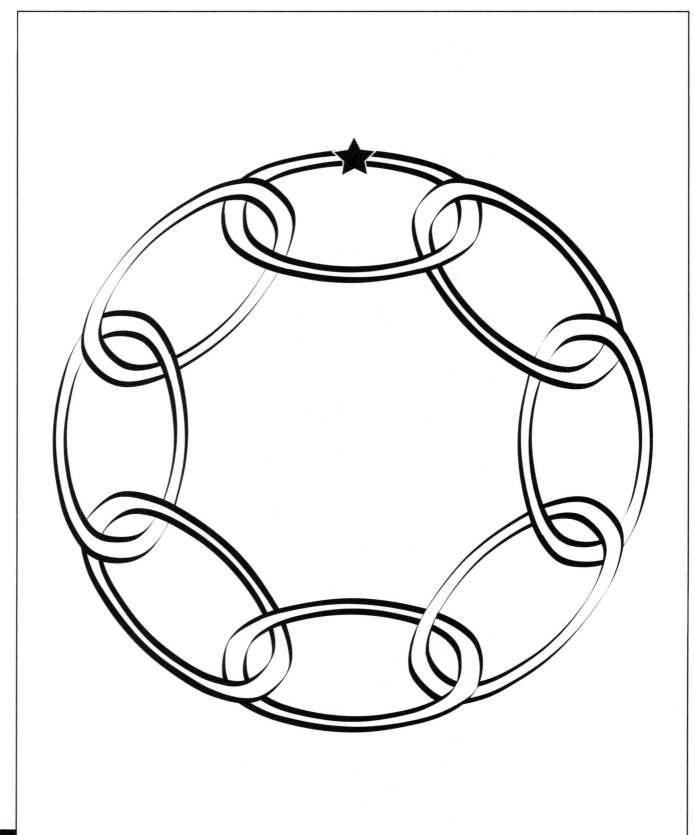

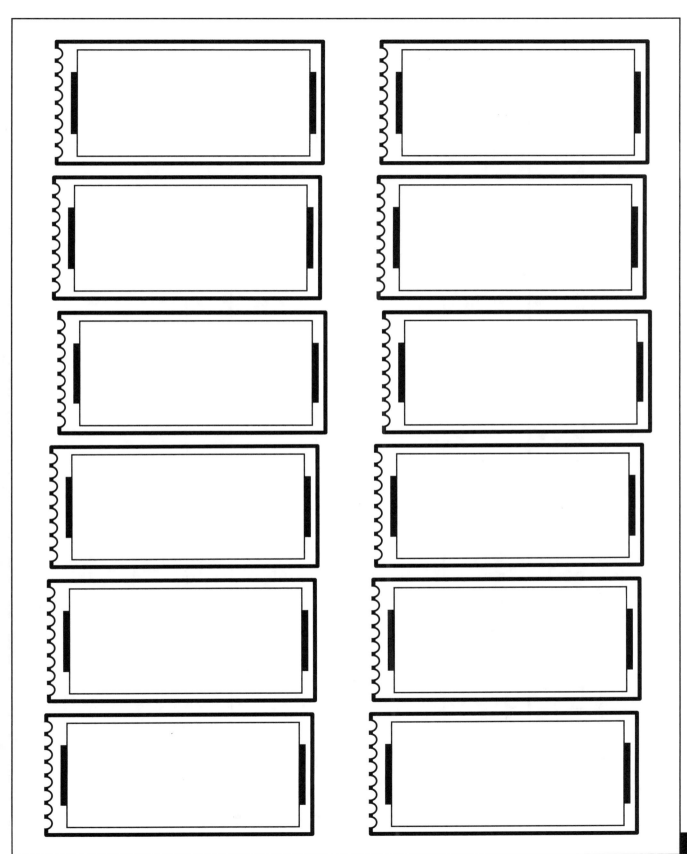

Name _____ Topic or Title _____

Read each statement below before you read the text and check I agree or I disagree in the columns on the left. After you have read the text, reread the statements and check I agree or I disagree in the columns on the right.

| Before reading | | Statements | After reading | |
I agree	I disagree		I agree	I disagree

Two facts I learned: 1. _____ 2. _____

Two questions I still need answered: 1. _____ 2. _____

One thing I'm sure about: _____

Name _____

Topic or Title _____

What I Might Know:

Facts I Can Show:

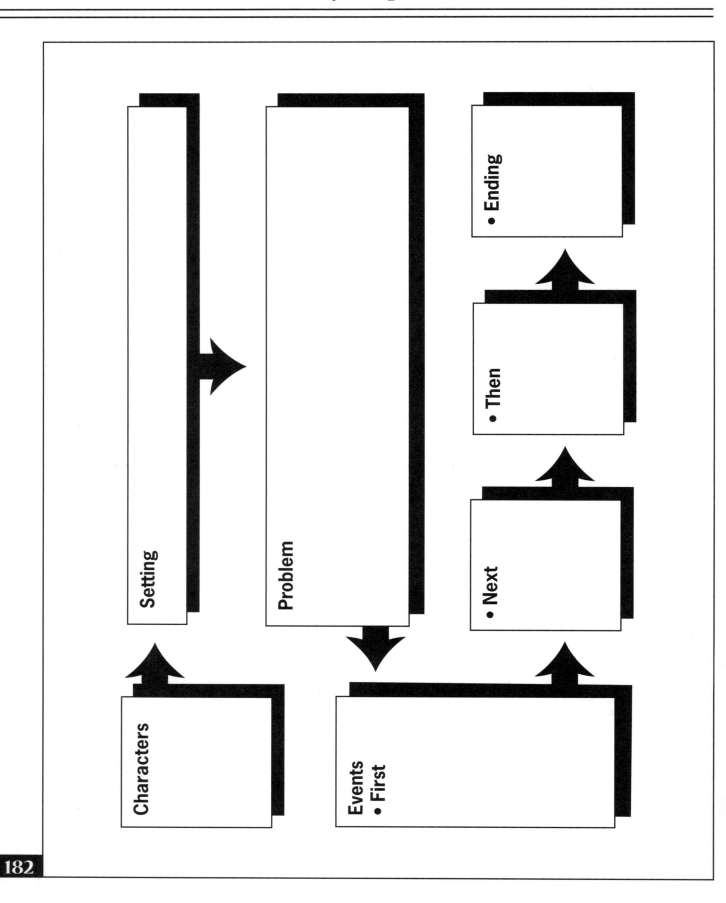

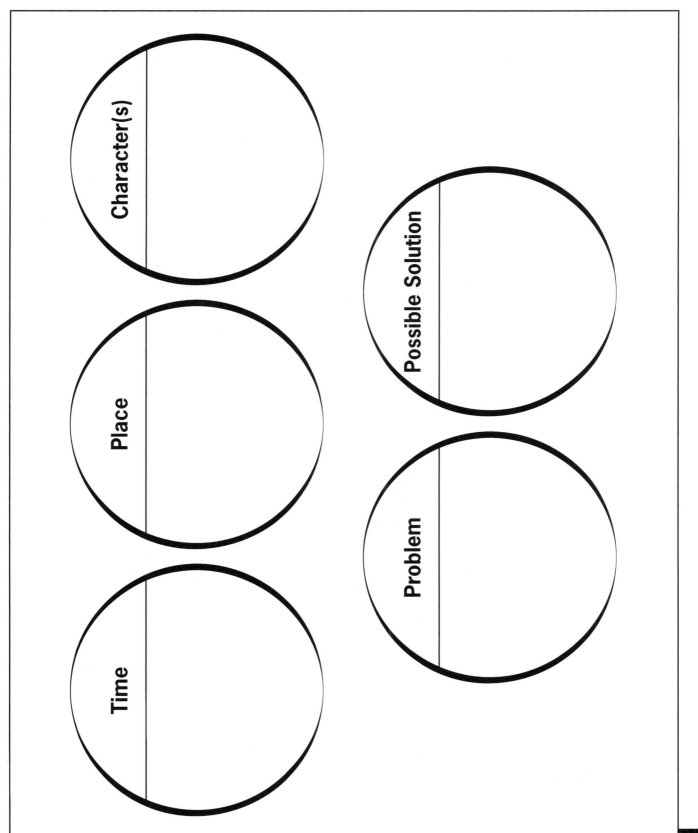

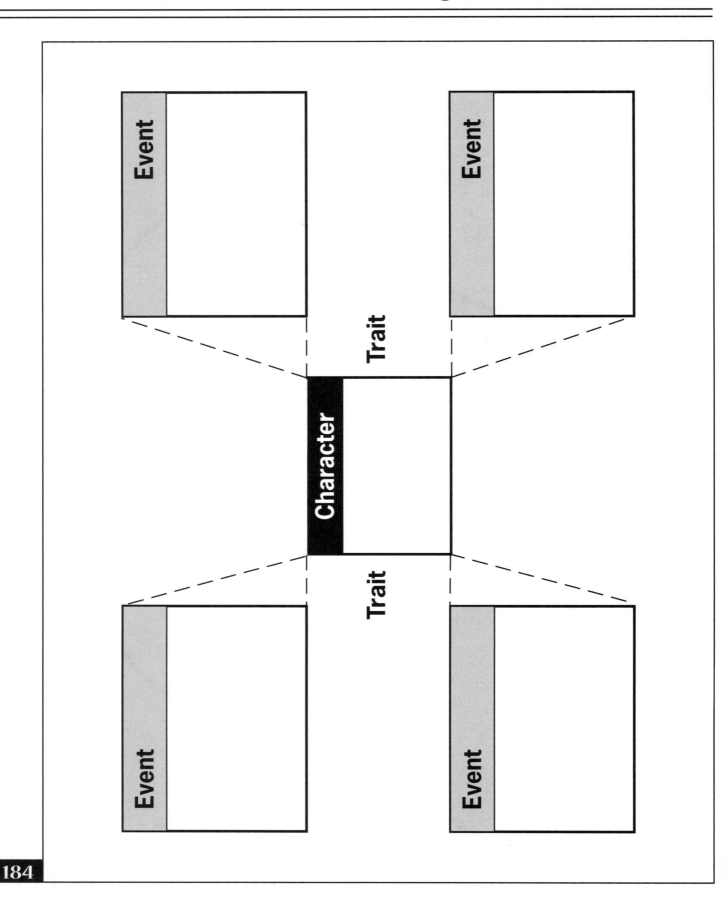

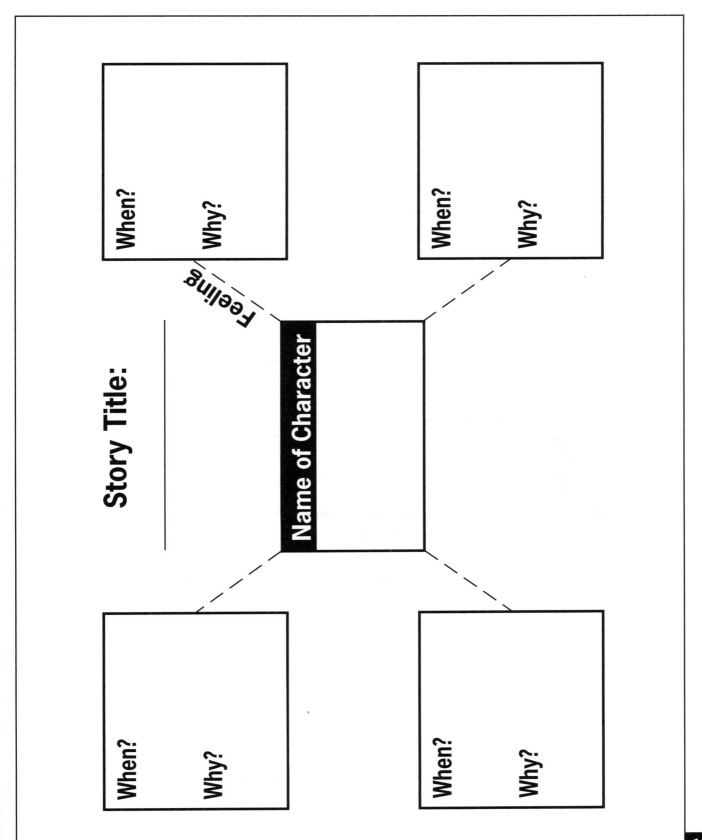

Story Title:

Name of Character

Feeling

When?

Why?

When?

Why?

When?

Why?

When?

Why?

185

DETAILS

+

MAIN IDEAS

Sequence Chain for

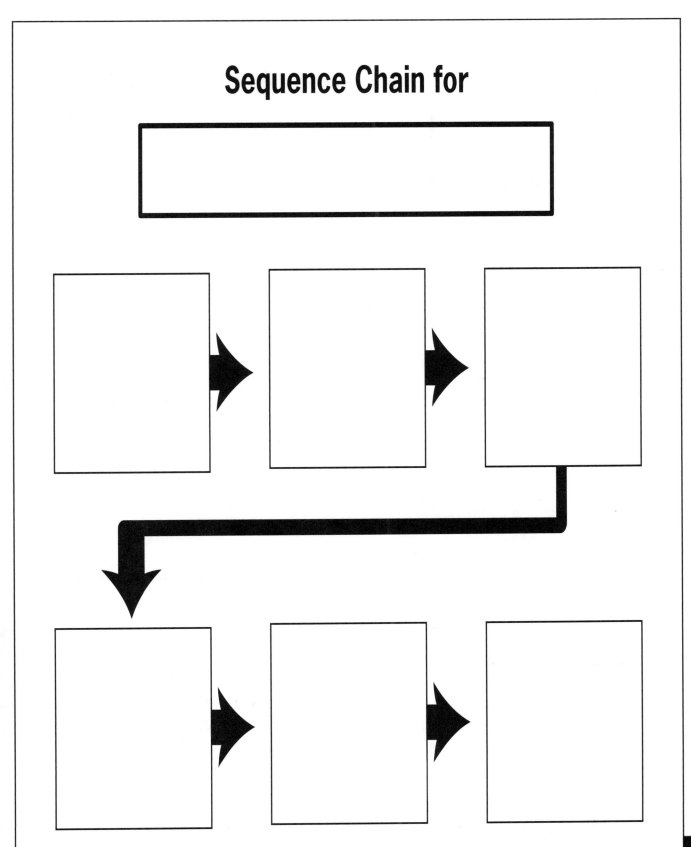

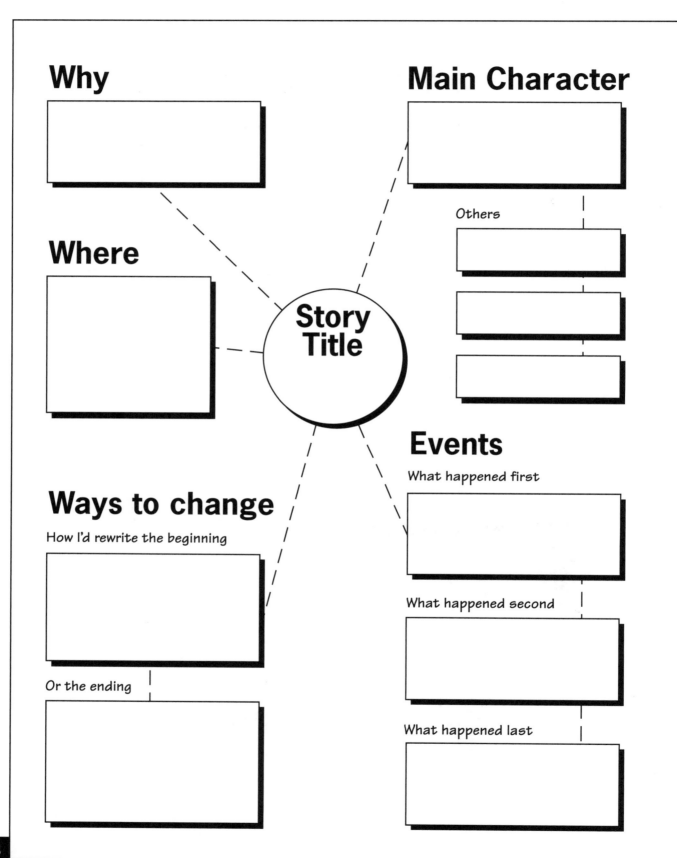

Why

Where

Main Character

Others

Story Title

Ways to change

How I'd rewrite the beginning

Or the ending

Events

What happened first

What happened second

What happened last

6						
5						
4						
3						
2						
1						

Draw	Perform	Compose a song
Write a poem	Make a poster	Dress up
Create a Venn diagram	Write a new ending	Change the setting and problem

AHA!
Connections

AHA!
Connections

Name: _____

As you read, jot down notes in the column on the left about anything in the text that makes you have an AHA! Moment. These can be words, characters, events, or ideas that spark a response or catch your eye. You may also sketch whatever it was in the text that made you say "AHA!" In the right-hand column, jot notes about the connections you made to your own life.

AHA! Moments	My Connections

Story Planning Pyramid

_____

Main character's name

_____

Two words
describing this person

_____

Three words
describing the setting or place

_____

Four words
describing an important event

_____

Five words
describing the main idea or the importance of this event

1	2	3	4	5	6	7	8	9	10	11	12
2	4	6	8	10	12	14	16	18	20	22	24
3	6	9	12	15	18	21	24	27	30	33	36
4	8	12	16	20	24	28	32	36	40	44	48
5	10	15	20	25	30	35	40	45	50	55	60
6	12	18	24	30	36	42	48	54	60	66	72
7	14	21	28	35	42	49	56	63	70	77	84
8	16	24	32	40	48	56	64	72	80	88	96
9	18	27	36	45	54	63	72	81	90	99	108
10	20	30	40	50	60	70	80	90	100	110	120
11	22	33	44	55	66	77	88	99	110	121	132
12	24	36	48	60	72	84	96	108	120	132	144

One yard

Three feet = one yard

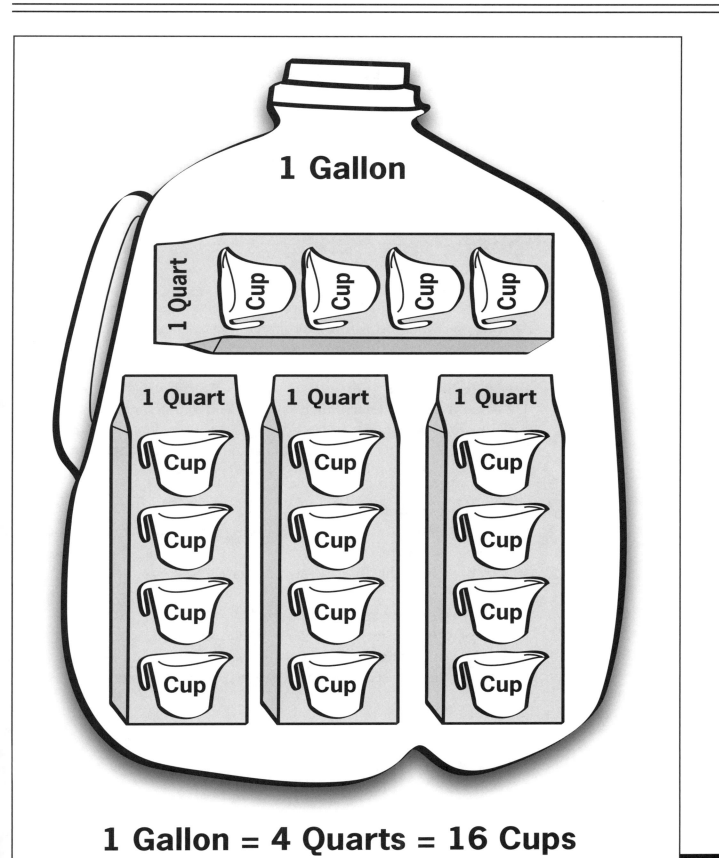

1 Gallon = 4 Quarts = 16 Cups

Teacher Resources

Web Sites

http://ies.ed.gov/ncee/wwc
The What Works Clearinghouse (WWC) is a U.S. Department of Education Web site designed by the Institute of Educational Sciences to provide educators with a central source of scientific evidence of what works in education.

http://literacymatrix.com
The Arkansas Literacy Intervention Matrix site offers a "best practices" research-based approach to maximizing literacy success for all students. You'll find comprehensive lists of tiered interventions and intensive strategies to facilitate literacy. See the K–4 modification checklist for more great ideas.

http://progressmonitoring.net
The Research Institute on Progress Monitoring at the University of Minnesota is developing a system for evaluating the effects of individualized instruction on student progress within the general education curriculum.

www.bestevidence.org
BEE is the center for data-driven reform in education at Johns Hopkins University. The site offers summaries of current research findings on educational programs as well as full-text reviews of educational topics.

www.fcrr.org
The Florida Center for Reading Research Web site offers research-based information and interventions for struggling readers.

www.interventioncentral.org
Intervention Central has intervention ideas, plus other tools for educators to support intervention and assessment.

www.k8accesscenter.org/index.php
The Access Center is a site dedicated to enhancing access to the general education curriculum for students with disabilities. Resources focus on core content areas—language arts, math, and science—and include instructional strategies to provide students with disabilities access to rigorous academic content.

www.mathwire.com/whohas/whohas.html
Mathwire.com is a great place to find standards-based math activities. You'll find all kinds of *I am/who is* and *I have/who has* decks of cards you can download as PDFs.

www.nationalreadingpanel.org
The National Reading Panel publishes important research findings for parents, teachers, and school administrators. This site is an excellent resource for current research about reading instruction.

www.nrcld.com
The National Research Center on Learning Disabilities site has free, research-based articles that are designed to answer teachers' questions about specific learning disabilities and RTI.

www.RTI4success.org
This is the new site for the National Center on Response to Intervention. It offers a comprehensive online library of RTI topics, discussion forums, and more.

www.studentprogess.org
The National Center on Student Progress Monitoring provides assistance to states and districts and disseminates information about scientifically based student progress monitoring practices proven to work in academic content areas for grades K–5.

www.teachingmadeeasier.com
Designed to save teachers time, this site has a large database of words and pictures for creating differentiated activities and blackline masters. You can also use your own word lists. Choose from eight languages to help ESOL students.

Bibliography

Allington, R. (2005). *What Really Matters for Struggling Readers: Designing Research-Based Programs.* Boston, MA: Allyn & Bacon.

Armbruster, B., F. Lehr, and J. Osborn. (2001). *Put Reading First: The Research Building Blocks for Teaching Children to Read.* Partnership for Reading. www.nifl.gov/partnershipforreading

Bender, W. and C. Shores. (2007). *Response to Intervention: A Practical Guide for Every Teacher.* Thousand Oaks, CA: Corwin Press.

Brown-Chidsey, R. and M.W. Steege. (2005). *Response to Intervention: Principles and Strategies for Effective Practice.* New York: Guilford Press.

Fuchs, D. et al. (2003). "Responsiveness-to-Intervention: Definitions, Evidence, and Implications for the Learning Disabilities Construct." *Learning Disabilities Research & Practice,* 18, no. 3 (2003): 157–171.

Goodman, G. (1995). *I Can Learn!* Peterborough, NH: Crystal Springs Books.

———. (1998). *More I Can Learn!* Peterborough, NH: Crystal Springs Books.

Hall, S. (2006). *I've DIBEL'd, Now What?* Frederick, CO: Sopris West.

Kovaleski, J. F. (2002). "Best Practices in Operating Prereferral Intervention Teams." In Thomas, A. and Grimes, J. (eds.) Best Practices in School Psychology IV (pp. 645–656.) Washington, DC: National Association of School Psychologists.

"Making a Difference Means Making It Different: Honoring Children's Rights to Excellent Reading Instruction." Position paper of the International Reading Association. (March, 2000). www.reading.org

National Reading Panel. (2000). *Teaching Children to Read: An Evidence-Based Assessment of the Scientific Research Literature on Reading and Its Applications for Reading Instruction.* Washington, DC: National Institute of Child Health and Human Development (NICHD).

"Response to Intervention: NASDSE and CASE White Paper on RTI." (May 2006) National Association of State Directors of Special Education and the Council of Administrators of Special Education. www.nasdse.org

Speece, D.L., L.P. Case, and D.E. Molloy. (2003) "Responsiveness to General Education Instruction as the First Gate to Learning Disabilities Identification." *Learning Disabilities Research and Practice*, 18, no. 3: 147–156.

Tomlinson, C. (2001). *How to Differentiate Instruction in Mixed-Ability Classrooms*. Alexandria, VA: Association for Supervision and Curriculum Development.

"The Unique Role of Special Education and Special Educators." Council for Exceptional Children: Position on Response to Intervention (RTI): 10/07. www.cec.sped.org/Policy&Advocacy/CECProfessionalPolicies

Index

Also by
Gretchen Goodman

I Can Learn!
Strategies and Activities for Gray-Area Children

Inclusive Classrooms A to Z

More I Can Learn!
Strategies and Activities for Gray-Area Children

The More Ways You Teach,
The More Students You Reach
(with Char Forsten, Jim Grant, Betty Hollas,
and Donna Whyte)

Bring Gretchen Goodman right to your
school for on-site training!
To learn how, call (877) 388-2054.

To order RTI documentation folders,
go to www.crystalsprings.com or call 1-800-321-0401.